POP ANTHOLOGY - BOOK 1
50 POP SONGS FOR ALL PIANO METHODS

ISBN 978-1-5400-1545-7

Visit Hal Leonard Online at
www.halleonard.com

Contact us:
Hal Leonard
7777 West Bluemound Road
Milwaukee, WI 53213
Email: info@halleonard.com

In Europe, contact:
Hal Leonard Europe Limited
42 Wigmore Street
Marylebone, London, W1U 2RN
Email: info@halleonardeurope.com

In Australia, contact:
Hal Leonard Australia Pty. Ltd.
4 Lentara Court
Cheltenham, Victoria, 3192 Australia
Email: info@halleonard.com.au

Beauty and the Beast
from BEAUTY AND THE BEAST

Music by Alan Menken
Lyrics by Howard Ashman
Arranged by Fred Kern

Flowing (♩ = 160)

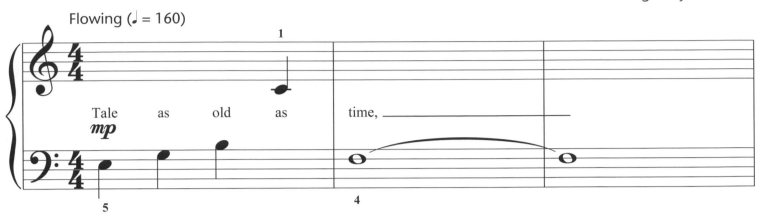

Tale as old as time,

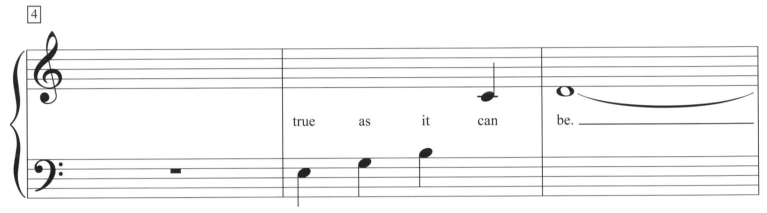

true as it can be.

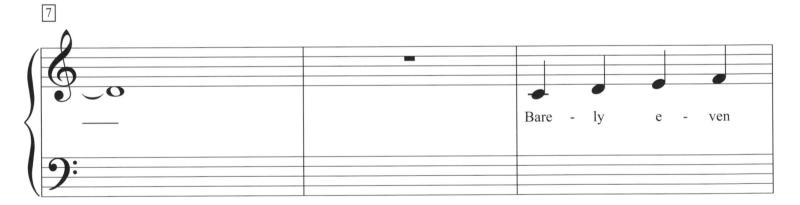

Bare - ly e - ven

Accompaniment (Student plays one octave higher than written.)

Flowing (♩ = 160)

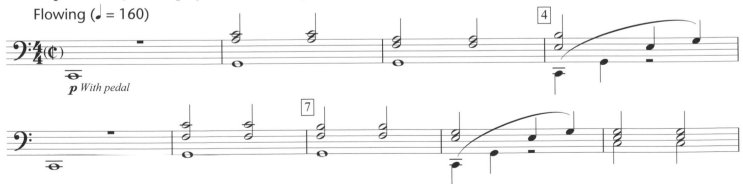

p With pedal

friends, then some - bod - y bends

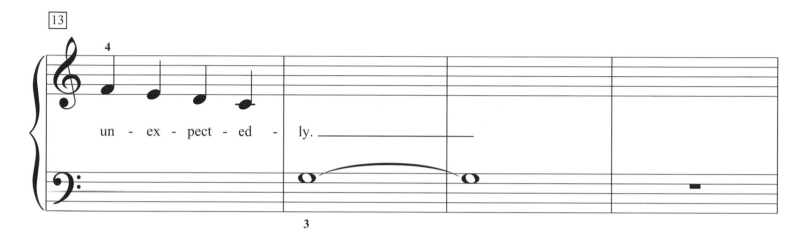

un - ex - pect - ed - ly.

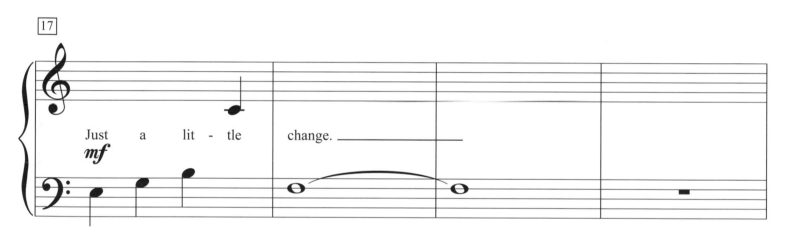

Just a lit - tle change.

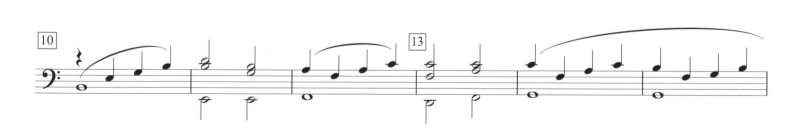

5

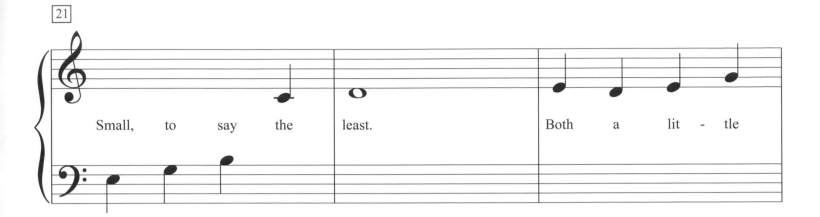

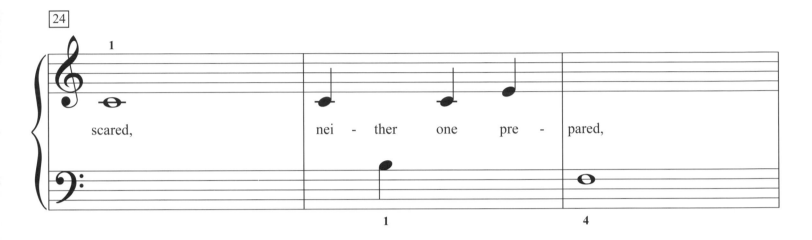

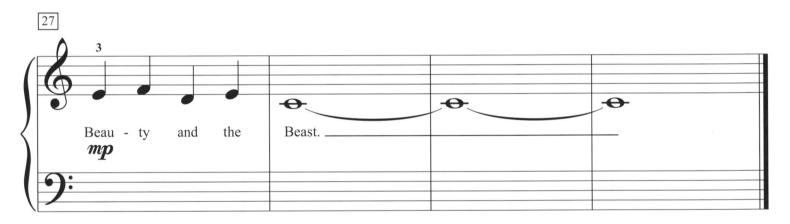

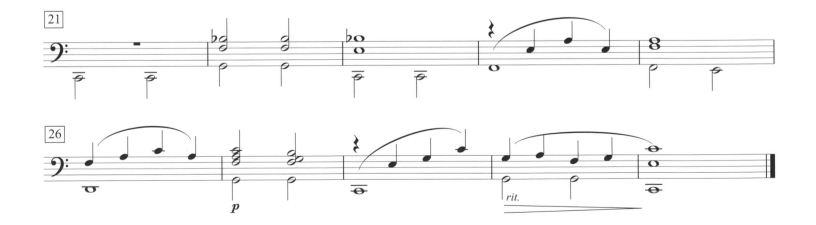

The Bells of Notre Dame

from THE HUNCHBACK OF NOTRE DAME

Music by Alan Menken
Lyrics by Stephen Schwartz
Arranged by Mona Rejino

With spirit (♩ = 146)

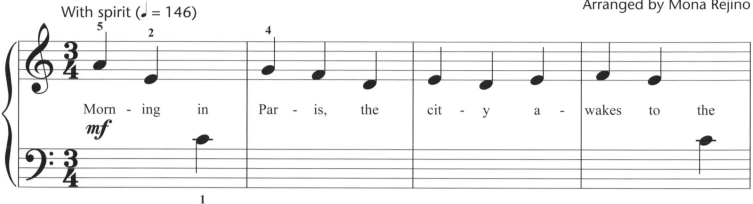

Morn - ing in Par - is, the cit - y a - wakes to the

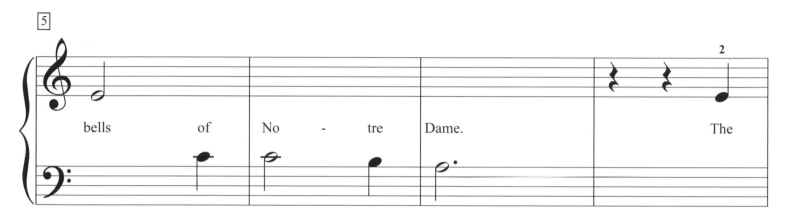

bells of No - tre Dame. The

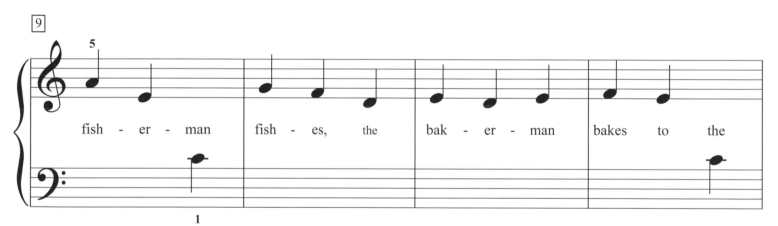

fish - er - man fish - es, the bak - er - man bakes to the

Accompaniment (Student plays one octave higher than written.)

With spirit (♩ = 146)

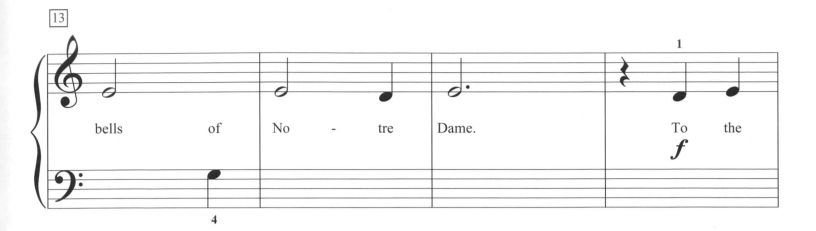

bells of No - tre Dame. To the **f**

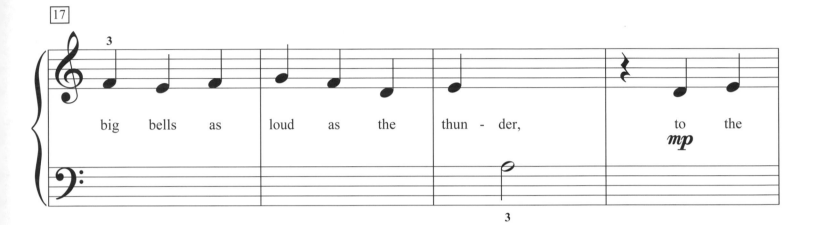

big bells as loud as the thun - der, to the **mp**

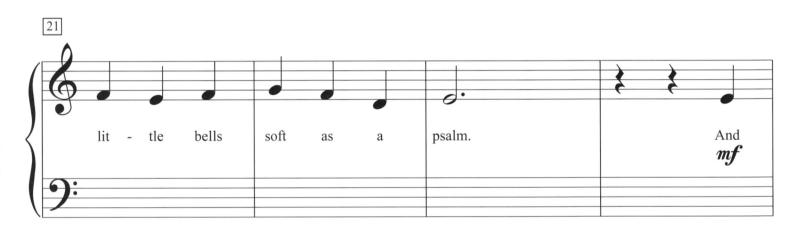

lit - tle bells soft as a psalm. And **mf**

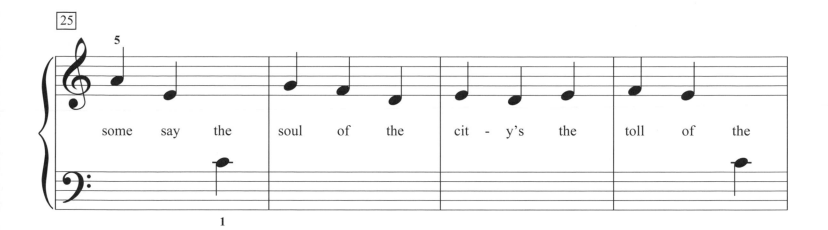

some say the soul of the cit-y's the toll of the

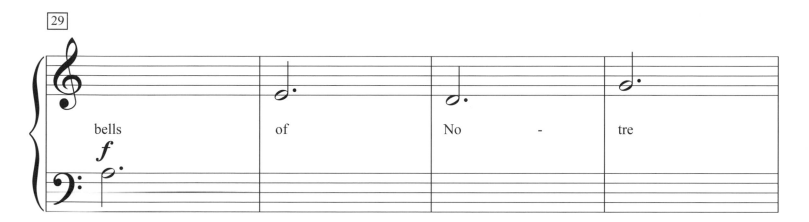

bells of No - tre

Dame.

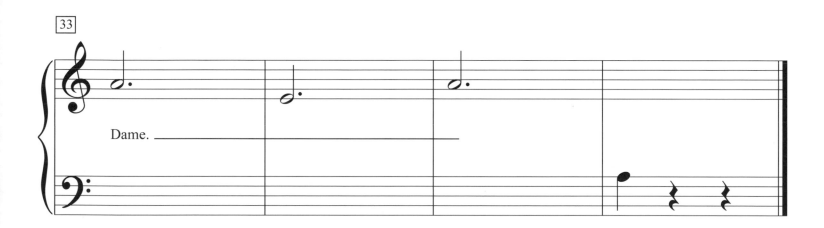

Can You Feel the Love Tonight

from THE LION KING

Music by Elton John
Lyrics by Tim Rice
Arranged by Mona Rejino

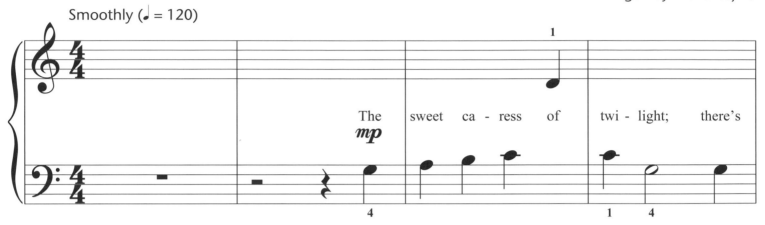

The sweet ca-ress of twi-light; there's

mag-ic ev-'ry-where. And with all this ro-man-tic

Accompaniment (Student plays one octave higher than written.)

Smoothly (♩ = 120)

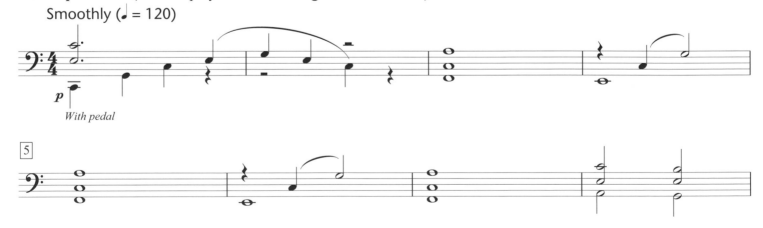

With pedal

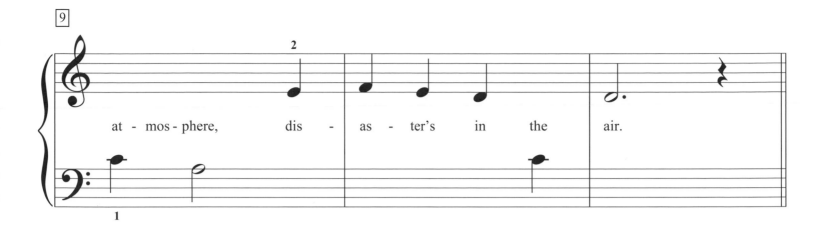

at - mos - phere,   dis - as - ter's in the   air.

mf Can   you   feel   the   love   to - night,

the peace the   eve - ning   brings? _____   The
you need - n't   look   too   far. _____

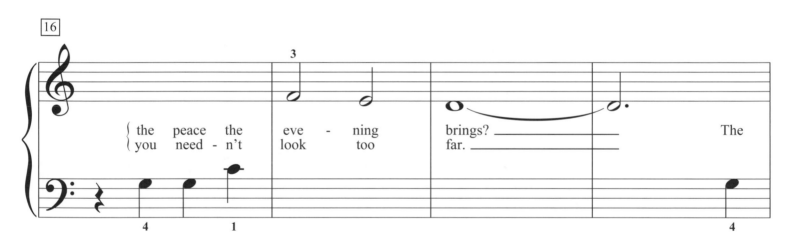

mp

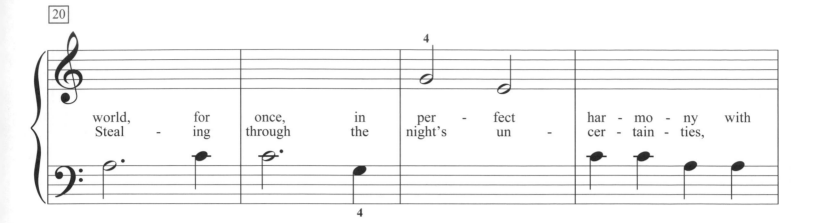

world, for once, in per - fect har - mo - ny with
Steal - ing through in the night's un - cer - tain - ties,

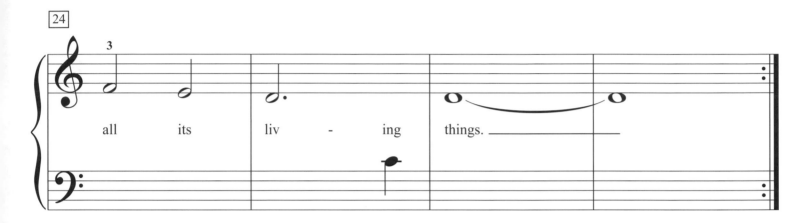

all its liv - ing things. _____

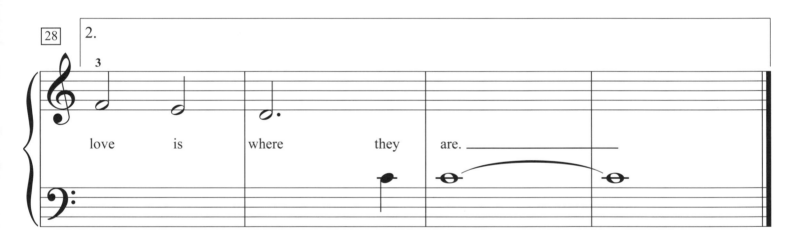

2.

love is where they are. _____

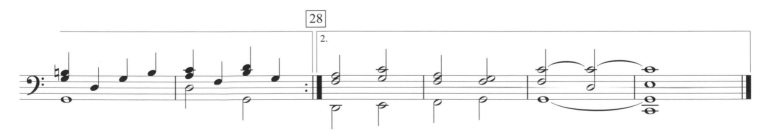

Circle of Life

from THE LION KING

Music by Elton John
Lyrics by Tim Rice
Arranged by Fred Kern

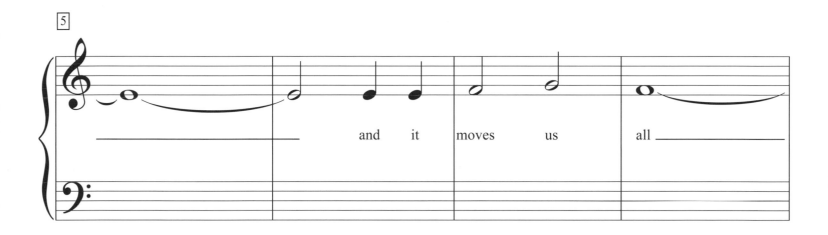

Accompaniment (Student plays one octave higher than written.)

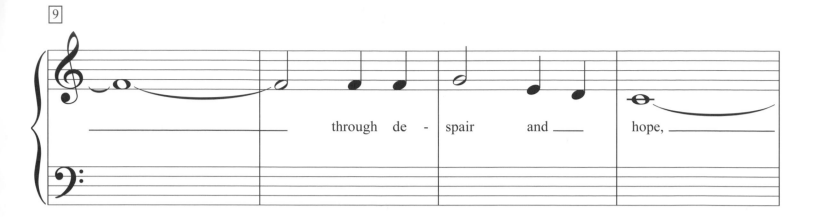

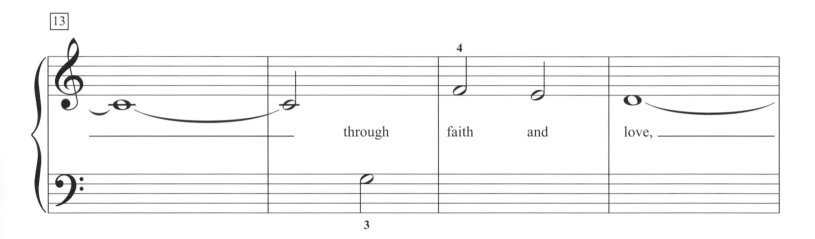

through de - spair and hope,

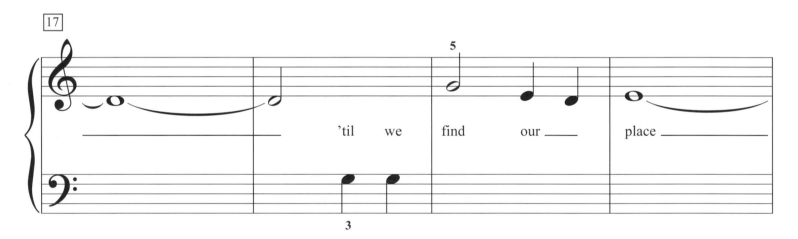

through faith and love,

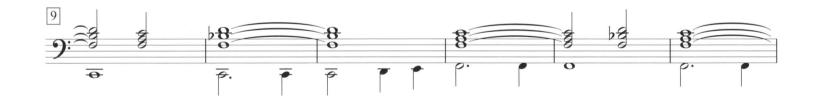

'til we find our place

cresc.

14

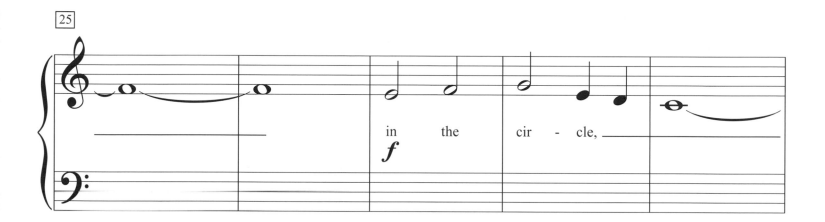

Feed the Birds

from MARY POPPINS

Words and Music by Richard M. Sherman
and Robert B. Sherman
Arranged by Fred Kern

Accompaniment (Student plays one octave higher than written.)

Happy Birthday to You

Words and Music by Mildred J. Hill
and Patty S. Hill
Arranged by Phillip Keveren

Hallelujah

Words and Music by
Leonard Cohen
Arranged by Fred Kern

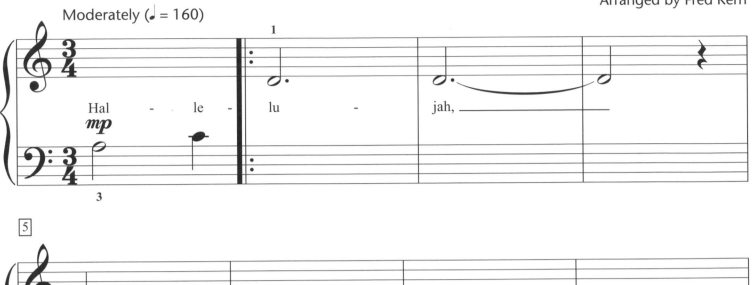

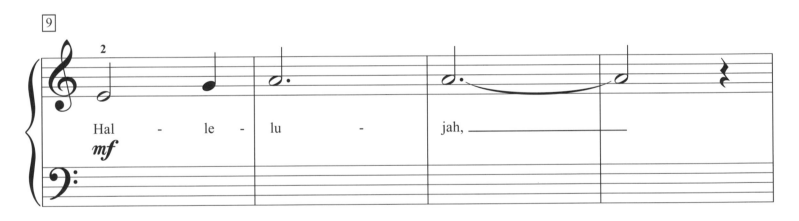

Accompaniment (Student plays one octave higher than written.)

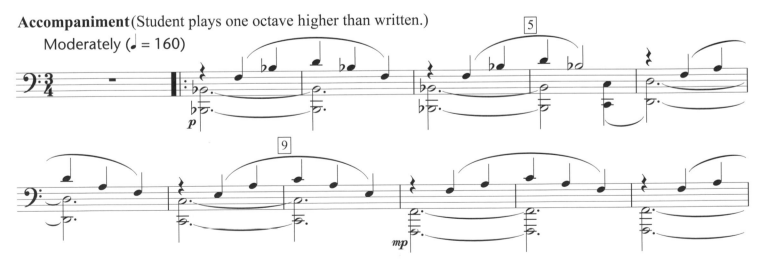

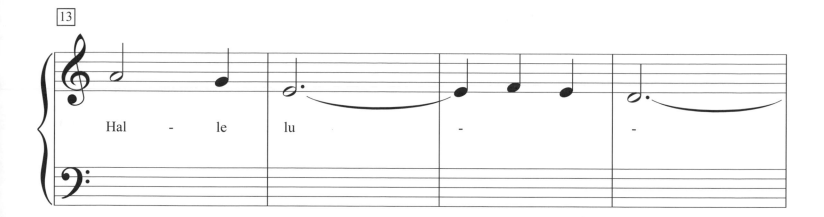

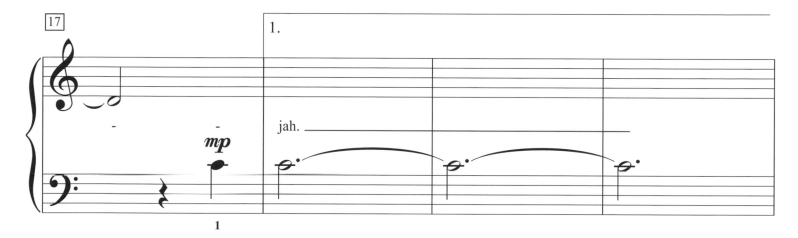

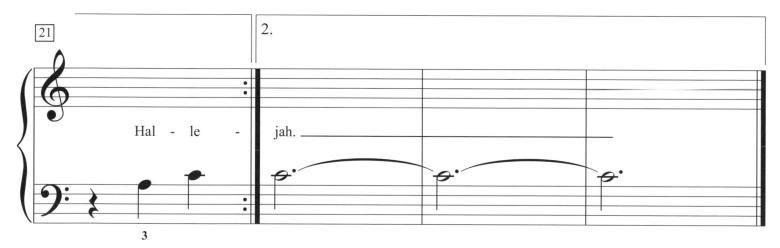

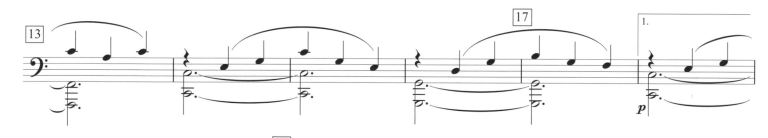

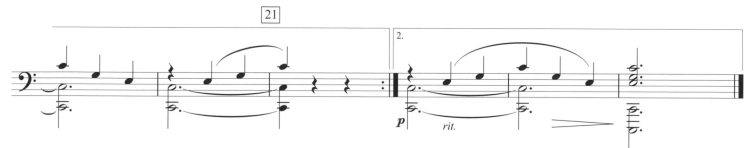

Love Is a Song

from BAMBI

Words by Larry Morey
Music by Frank Churchill
Arranged by Mona Rejino

Love is a song that nev - er ends.
Love is a song that that nev - er ends,

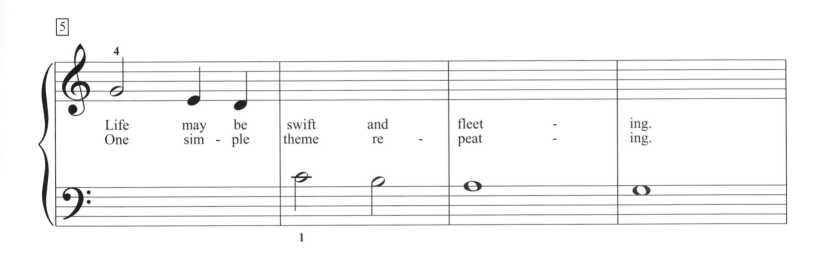

Life may be swift and fleet - ing.
One sim - ple theme and re - peat - ing.

Accompaniment (Student plays one octave higher than written.)

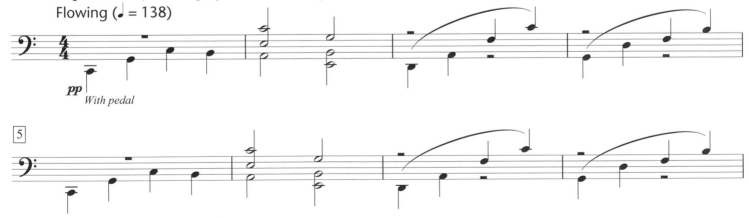

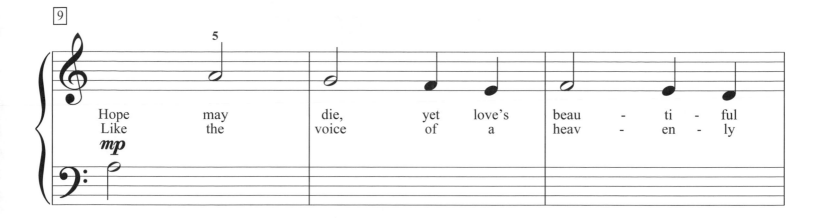

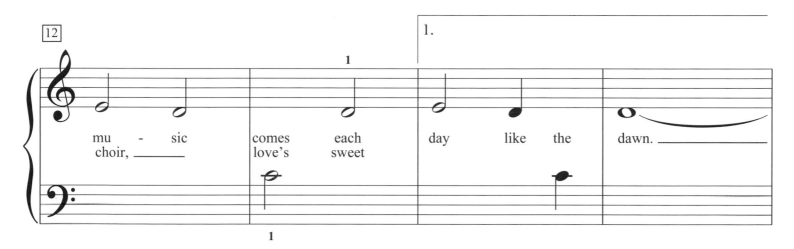

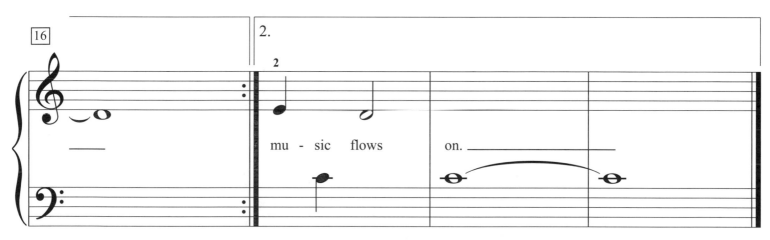

On Top of Spaghetti

Words and Music by Tom Glazer
Arranged by Phillip Keveren

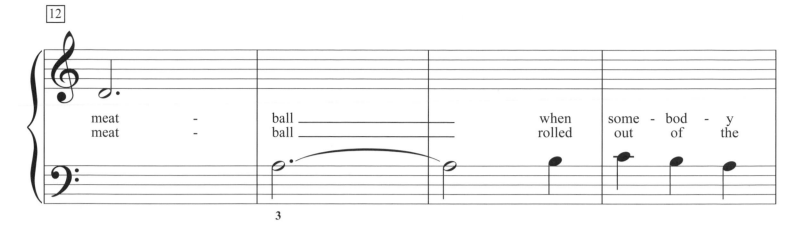

meat - ball when some - bod - y
meat - ball rolled out of the

3

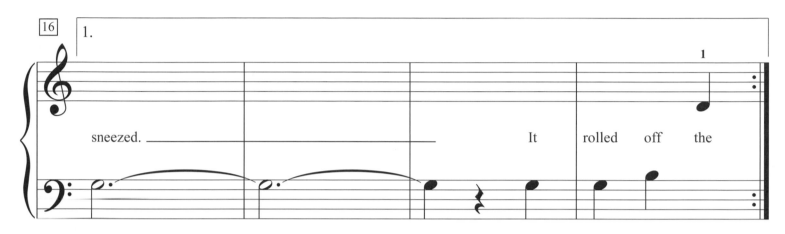

1.
sneezed. It rolled off the

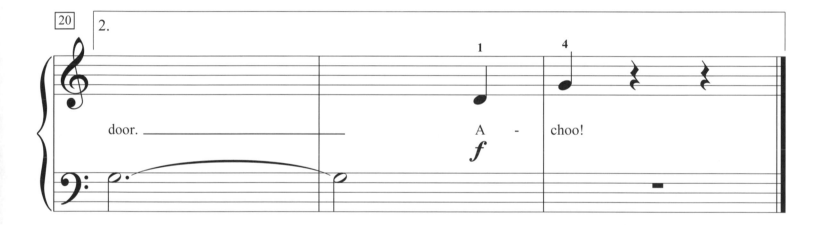

2.
door. A - choo!
f

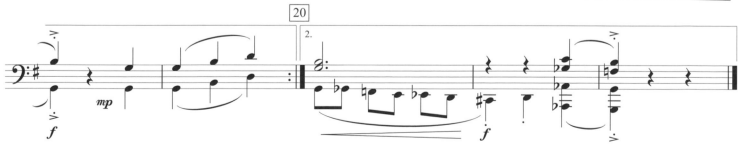

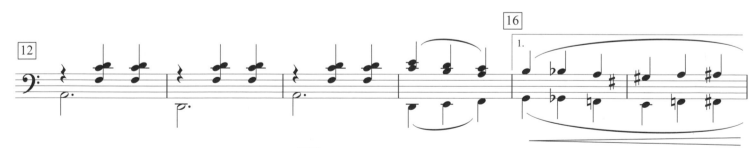

Pumpkin Song

Words and Music by
Jennifer Linn

Here's a fa - mous song I learned, I'm get - ting just a

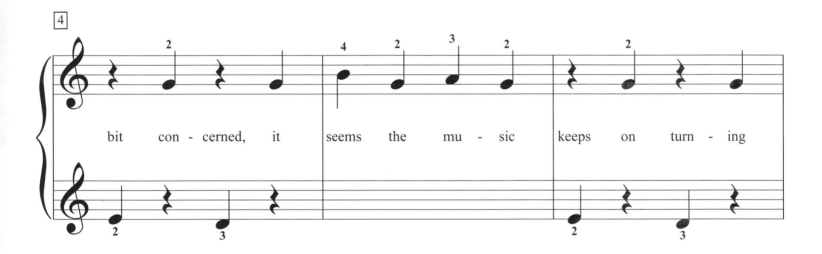

bit con - cerned, it seems the mu - sic keeps on turn - ing

Accompaniment (Student plays one octave higher than written.)

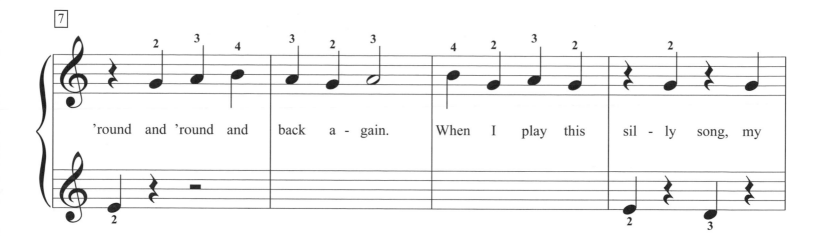

'round and 'round and back a - gain. When I play this sil - ly song, my

friends say, "Just don't play too long." This Pump - kin Song has

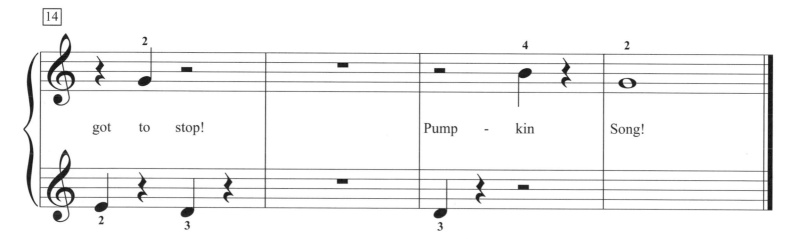

got to stop! Pump - kin Song!

25

Supercalifragilisticexpialidocious

from MARY POPPINS

Words and Music by Richard M. Sherman
and Robert B. Sherman
Arranged by Carol Klose

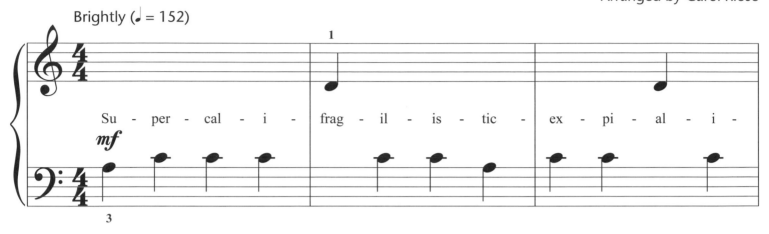

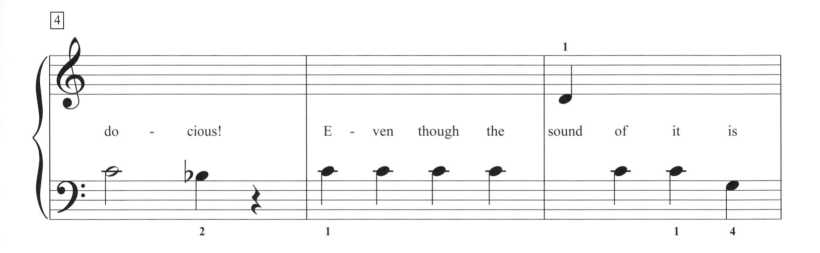

Accompaniment (Student plays one octave higher than written.)

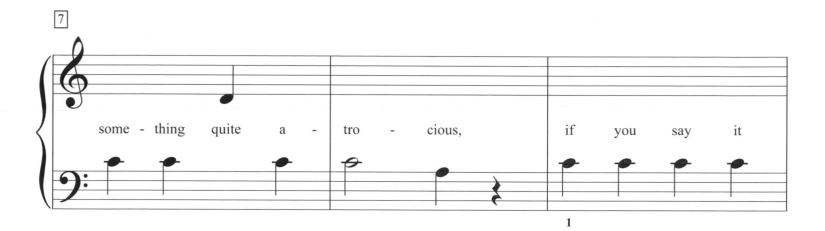

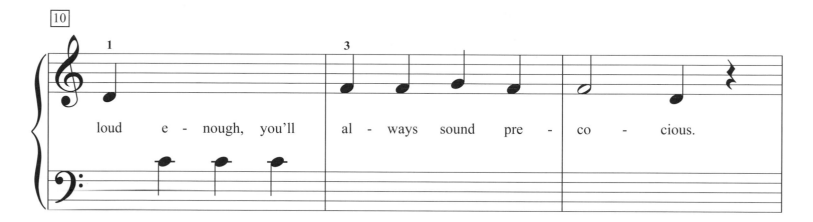

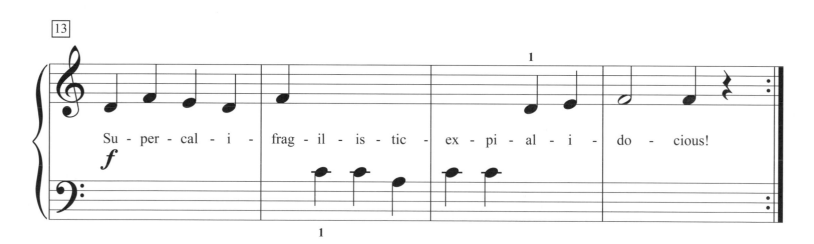

This Land Is Your Land

Words and Music by
Woody Guthrie
Arranged by Fred Kern

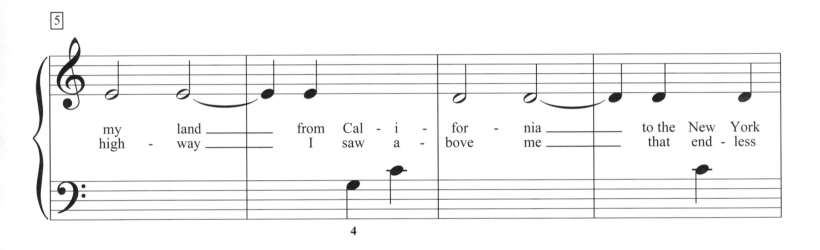

Accompaniment (Student plays one octave higher than written.)

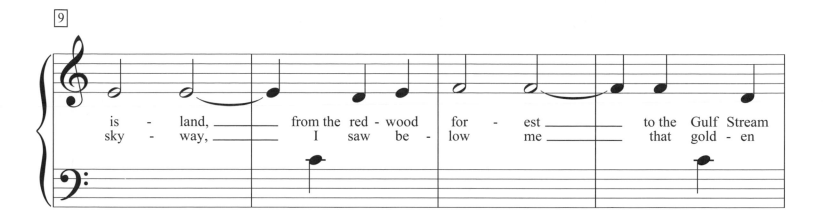

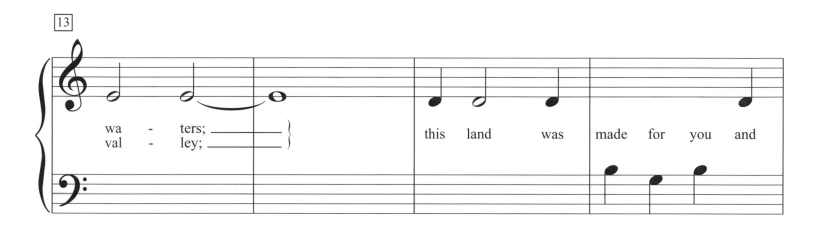

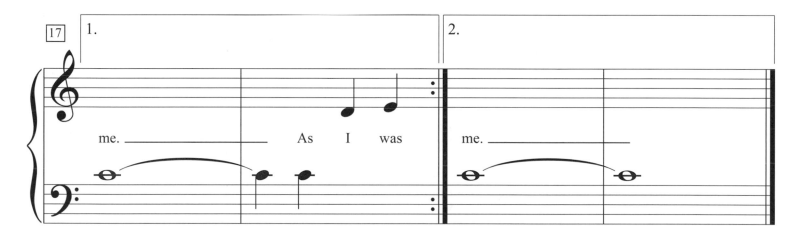

Mickey Mouse March

from THE MICKEY MOUSE CLUB

Words and Music by Jimmie Dodd
Arranged by Mona Rejino

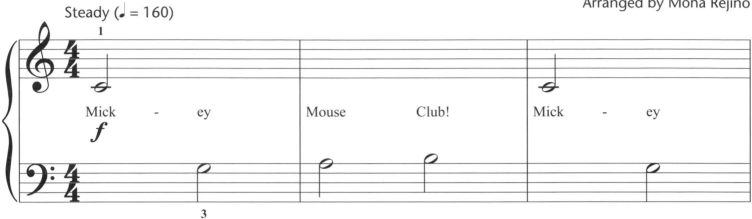

Mick - ey   Mouse   Club!   Mick - ey

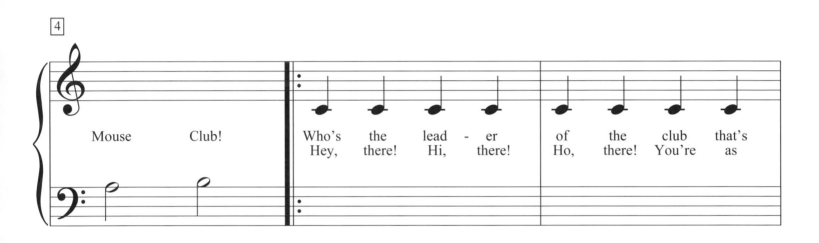

Mouse   Club!   Who's the lead - er   of the club that's
                          Hey, there! Hi, there!   Ho, there! You're as

Accompaniment (Student plays one octave higher than written.)

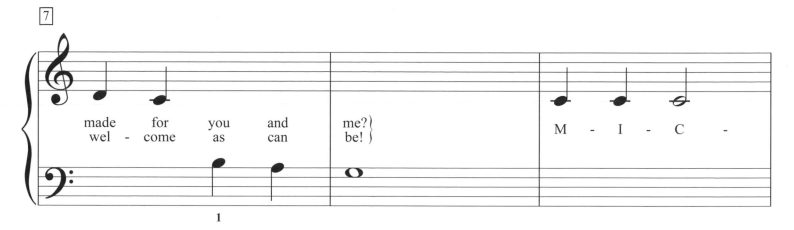

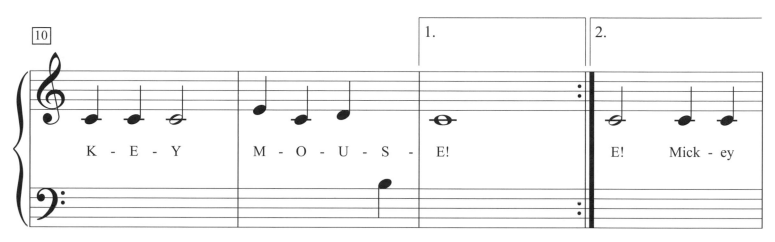

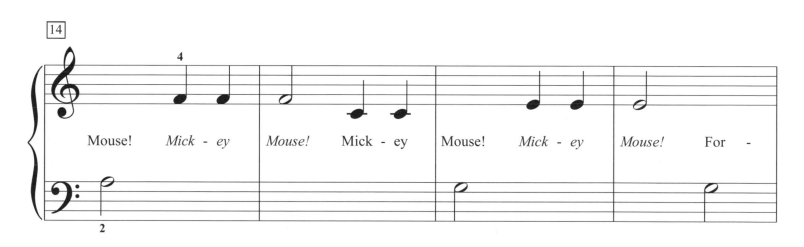

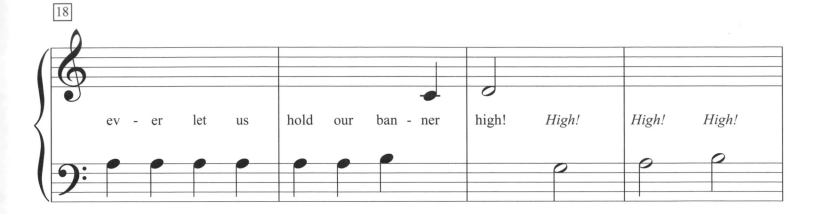

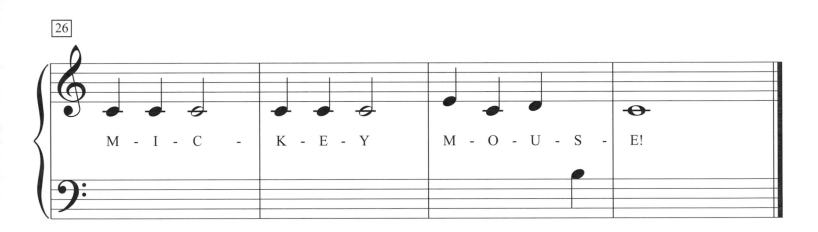

The Wonderful Thing About Tiggers

from THE MANY ADVENTURES OF WINNIE THE POOH

Words and Music by Richard M. Sherman
and Robert B. Sherman
Arranged by Phillip Keveren

With a bounce (♩. = 76)

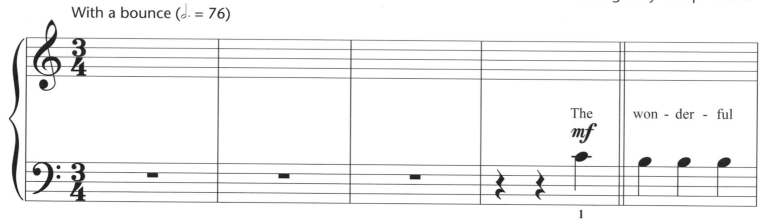

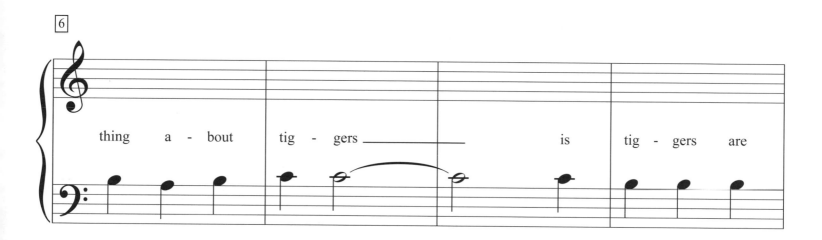

Accompaniment (Student plays one octave higher than written.)

With a bounce (♩. = 76)

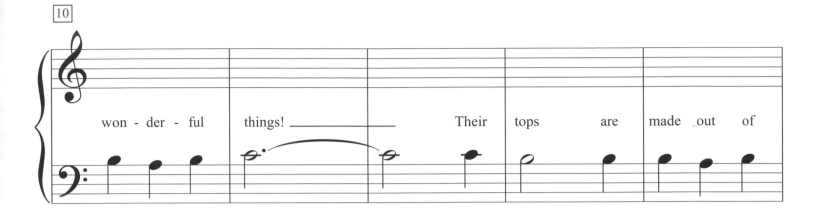

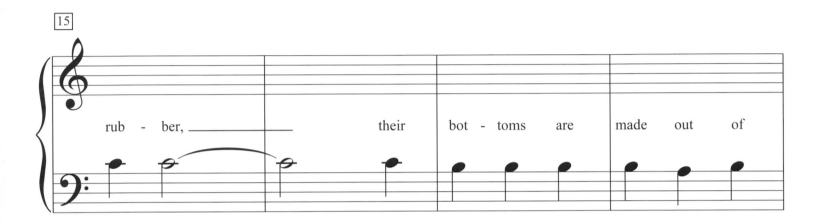

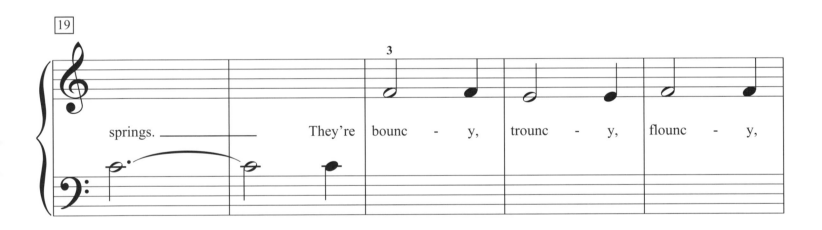

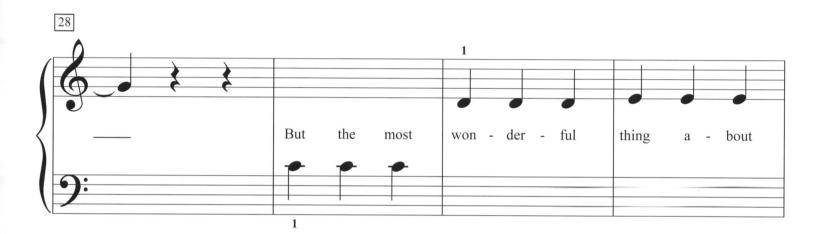

pounc - y, fun! Fun! Fun! Fun! Fun! _____

_____ But the most won - der - ful thing a - bout

tig - gers is I'm the on - ly one!

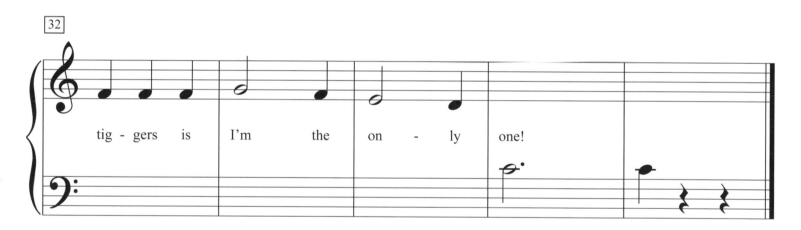

The Bare Necessities

from THE JUNGLE BOOK

Words and Music by
Terry Gilkyson
Arranged by Fred Kern

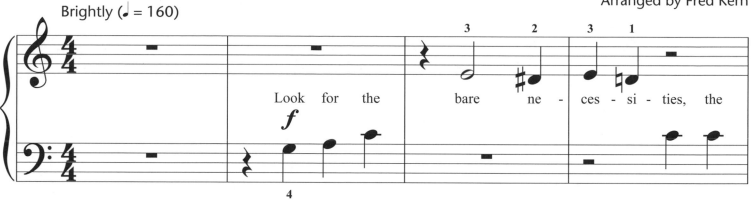

Brightly (♩ = 160)

f

Look for the bare ne - ces - si - ties, the

sim - ple bare ne - ces - si - ties. For - get a - bout your wor - ries and your

strife. I mean the bare ne - ces - si - ties, oh,

Accompaniment (Student plays one octave higher than written.)

Brightly (♩ = 160)

mf

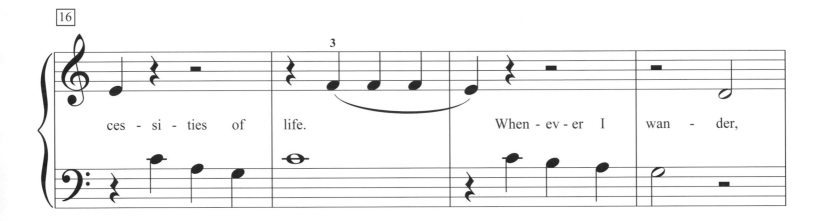

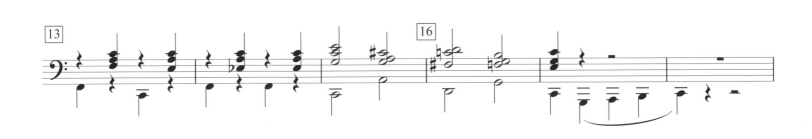

of my big home. The bees are buzz-in' in the

tree to make some hon-ey, just for me. The bare ne-

ces-si-ties of life will come to you. _____ *mp*

Bella Notte

from LADY AND THE TRAMP

Words and Music by Peggy Lee
and Sonny Burke
Arranged by Mona Rejino

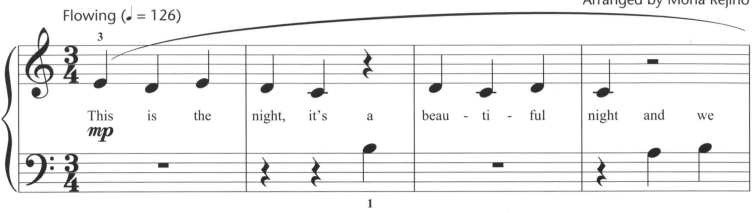

This is the night, it's a beau - ti - ful night and we

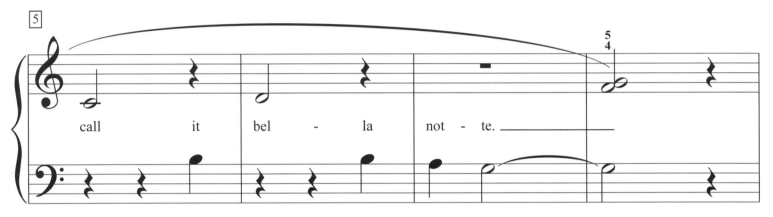

call it bel - la not - te. _____

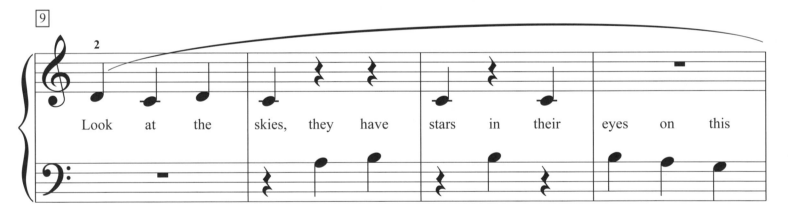

Look at the skies, they have stars in their eyes on this

Accompaniment (Student plays one octave higher than written.)

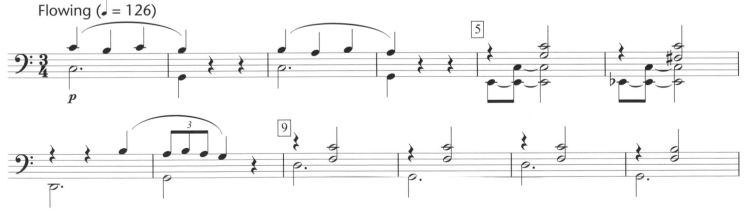

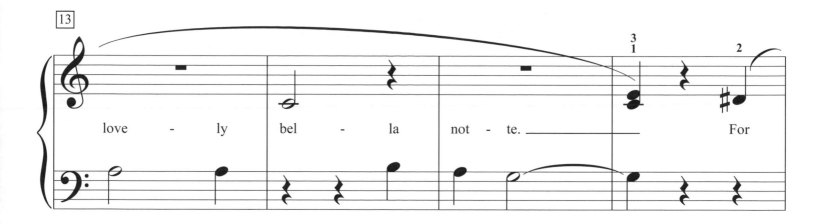

love - ly bel - la not - te. _____ For

this is the night and the hea - vens are right on this

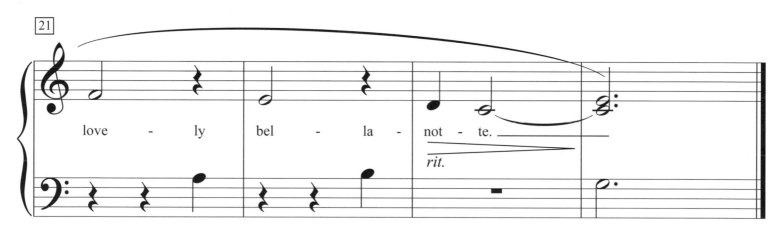

love - ly bel - la - not - te. _____
rit.

Castle on a Cloud

from LES MISÉRABLES

Music by Claude-Michel Schönberg
Lyrics by Alain Boublil, Jean-Marc Natel
and Herbert Kretzmer
Arranged by Carol Klose

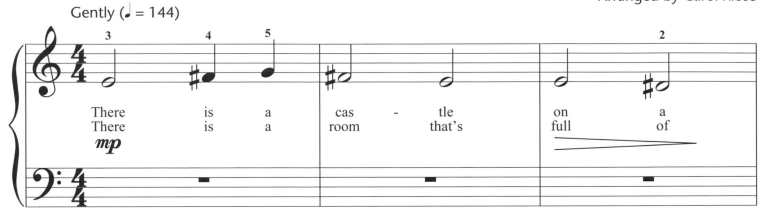

Accompaniment (Student plays one octave higher than written.)

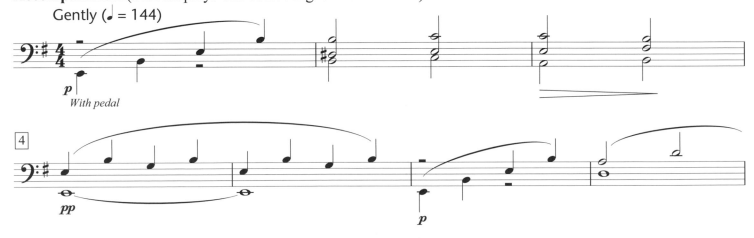

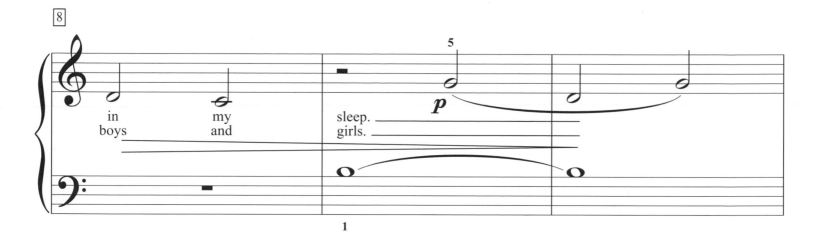

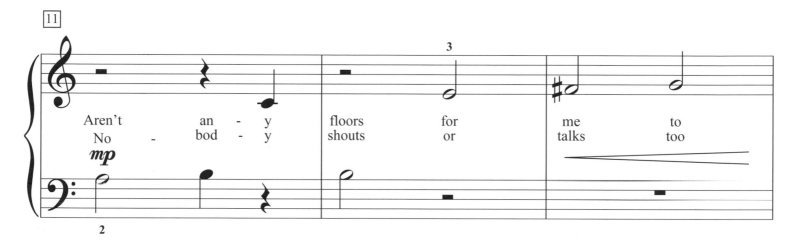

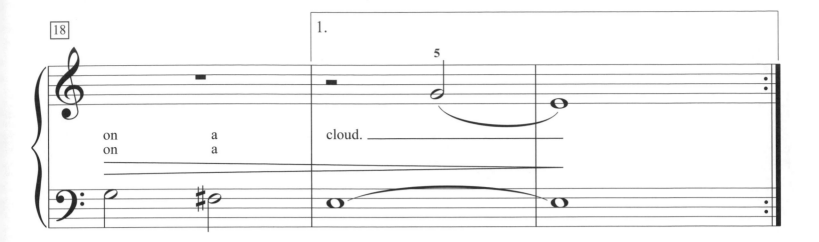

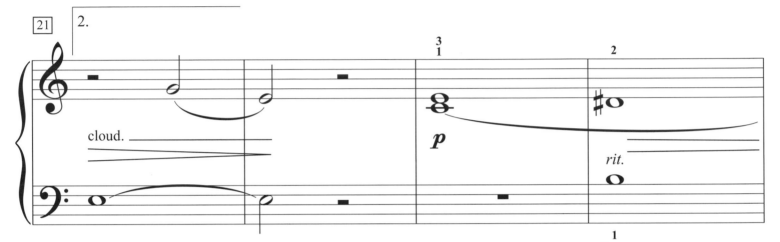

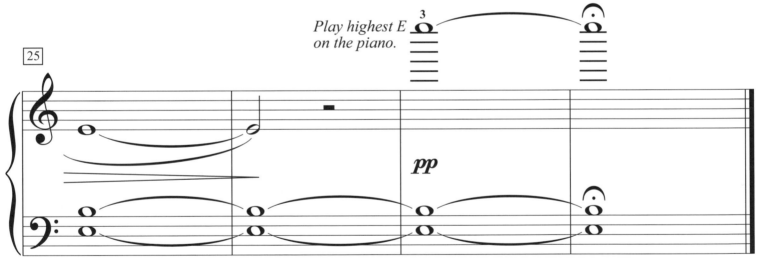

Climb Ev'ry Mountain

from THE SOUND OF MUSIC

Lyrics by Oscar Hammerstein II
Music by Richard Rodgers
Arranged by Mona Rejino

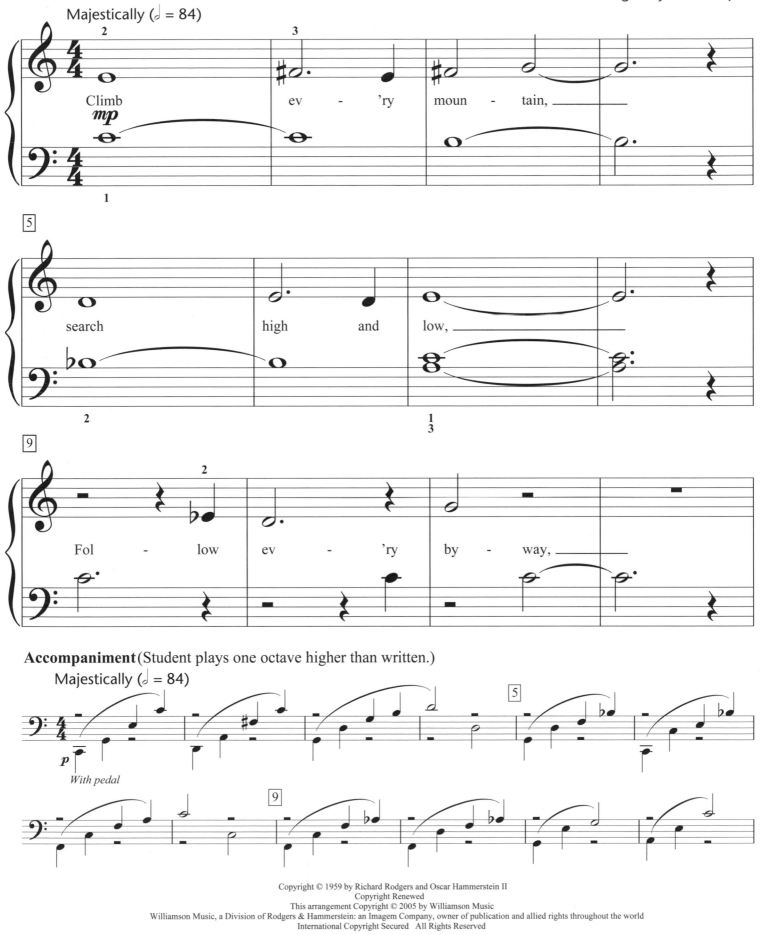

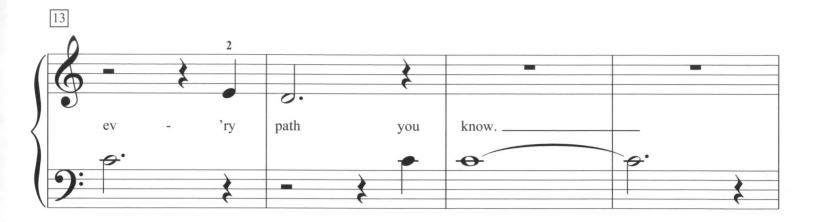

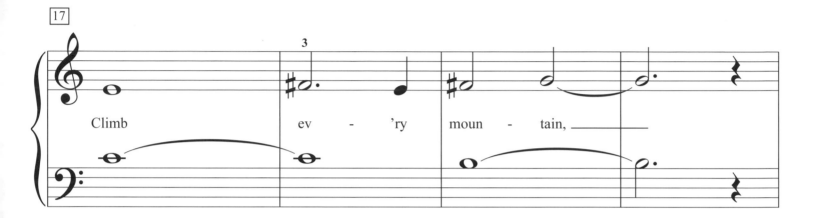

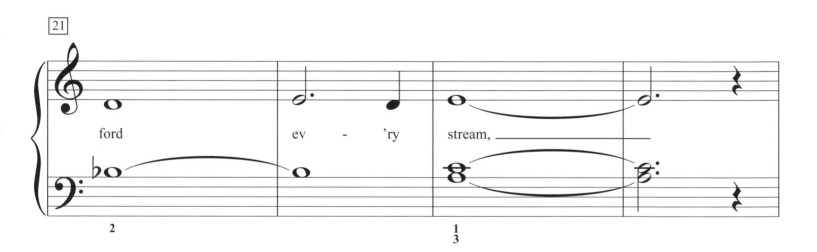

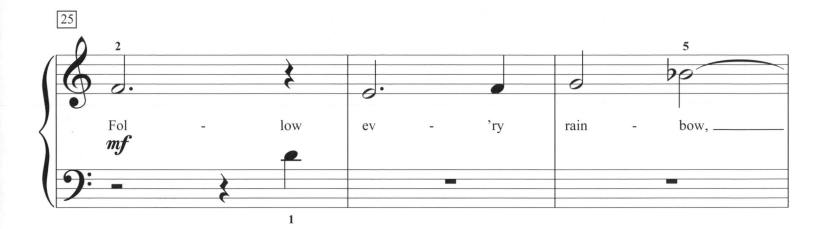

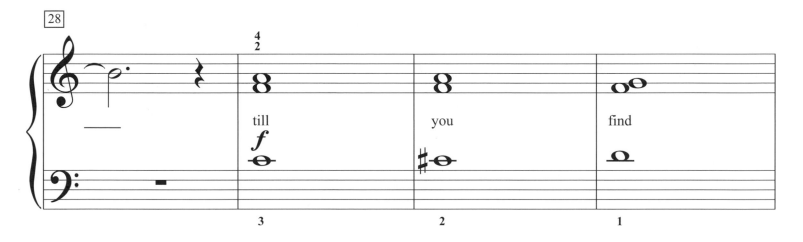

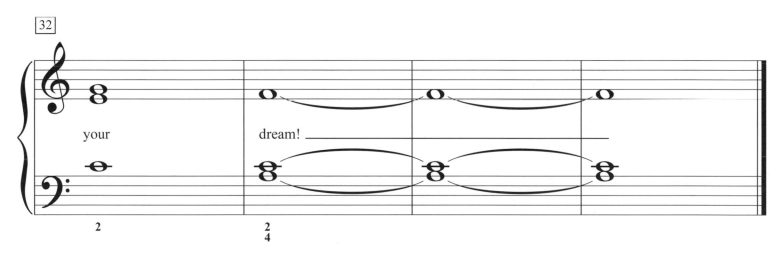

Ding-Dong! The Witch Is Dead

from THE WIZARD OF OZ

Lyric by E.Y. "Yip" Harburg
Music by Harold Arlen
Arranged by Phillip Keveren

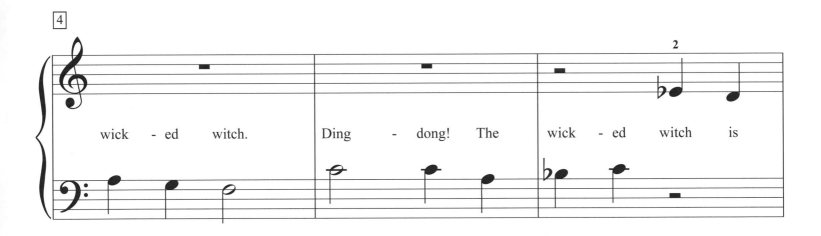

Accompaniment (Student plays one octave higher than written.)

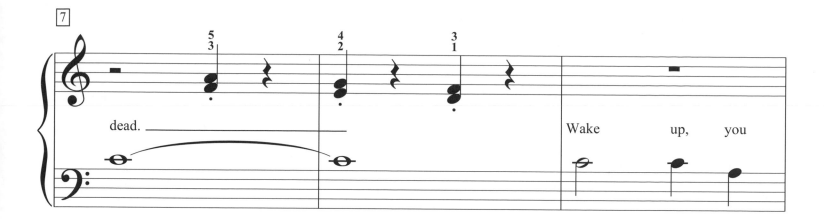

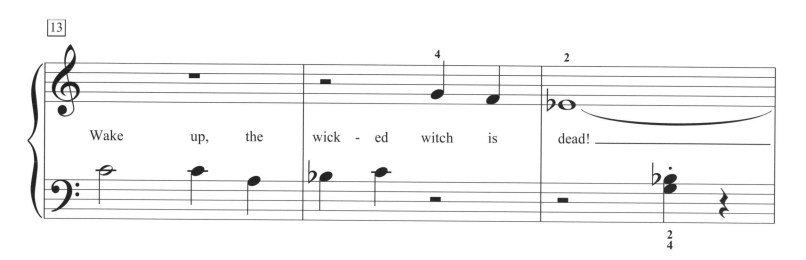

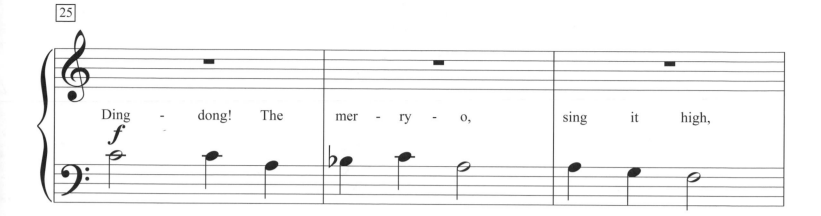

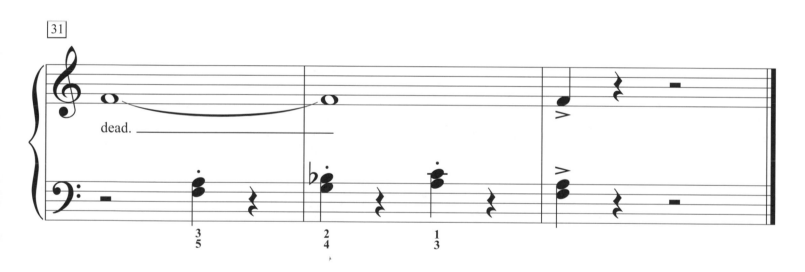

Ding - dong! The mer - ry - o, sing it high, sing it low, Let them know the wick - ed witch is dead. ____

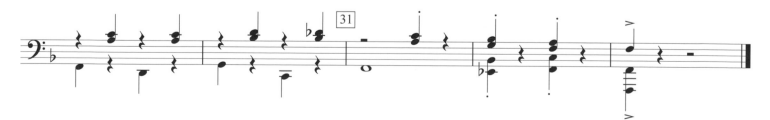

Edelweiss

from THE SOUND OF MUSIC

Lyrics by Oscar Hammerstein II
Music by Richard Rodgers
Arranged by Bill Boyd

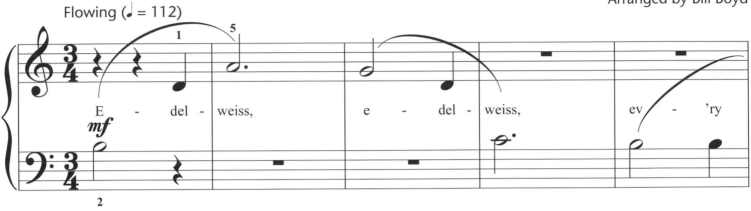

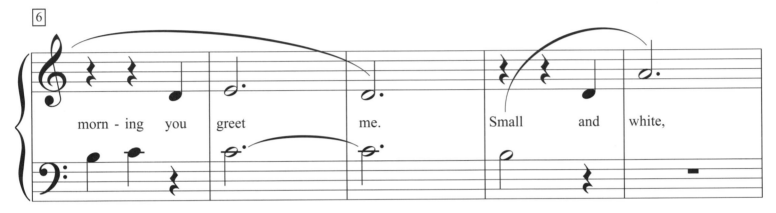

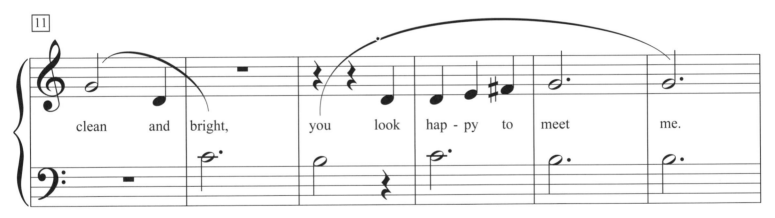

Accompaniment (Student plays one octave higher than written.)

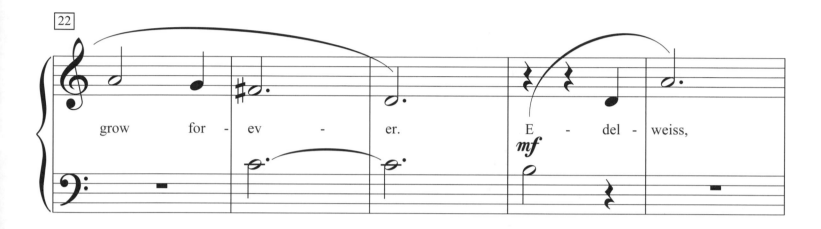

Hot Dog

Words and Music by John Flansburgh
and John Linnell
Arranged by Lynda Lybeck-Robinson

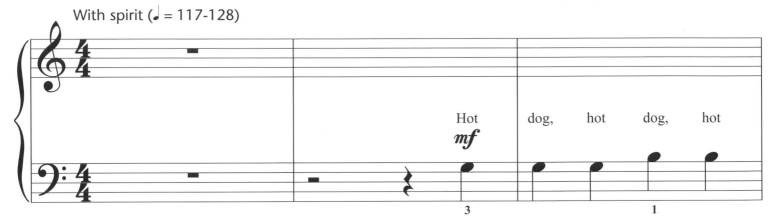

Accompaniment (Student plays one octave higher than written.)

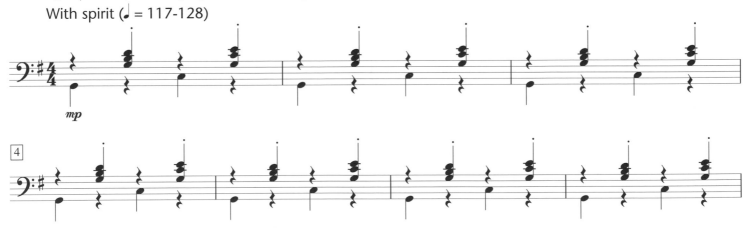

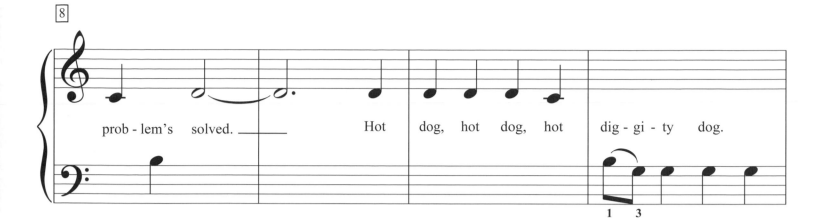

prob - lem's   solved. ____   Hot   dog,   hot   dog,   hot   dig - gi - ty   dog.

1   3

(Instrumental)

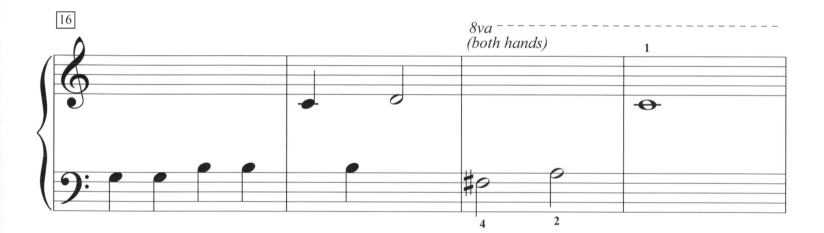

8va -
(both hands)

1

4   2

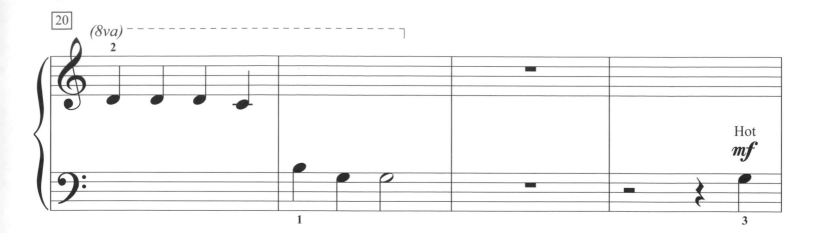

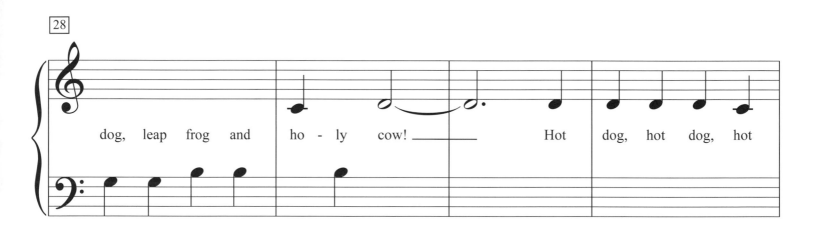

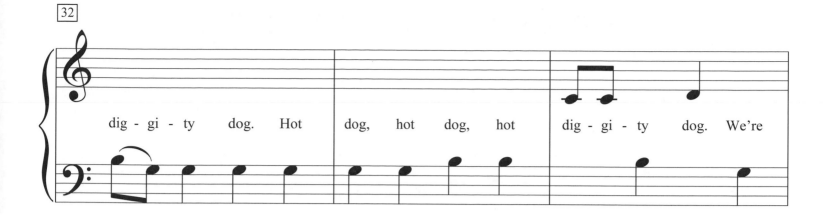

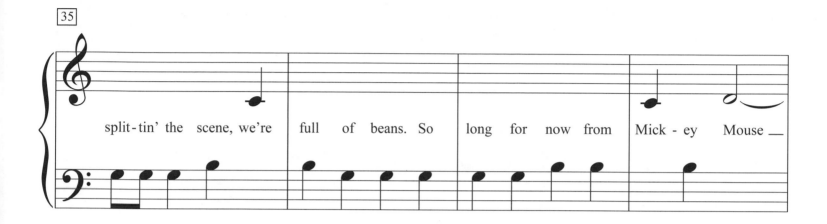

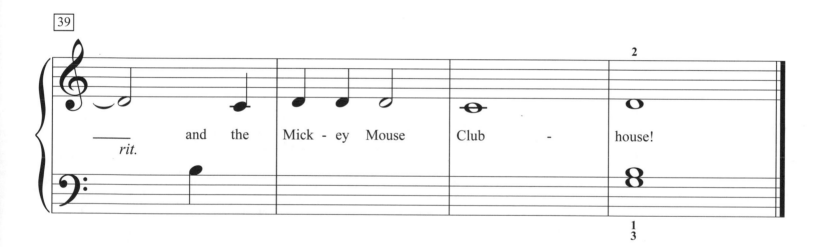

I Just Can't Wait to Be King

from THE LION KING

Music by Elton John
Lyrics by Tim Rice
Arranged by Mona Rejino

Accompaniment(Student plays one octave higher than written.)

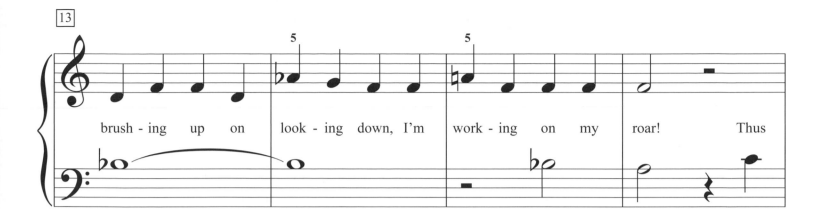

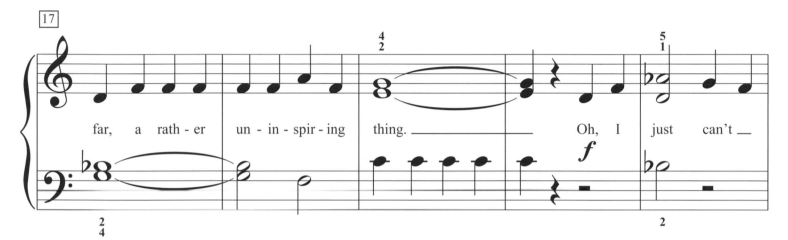

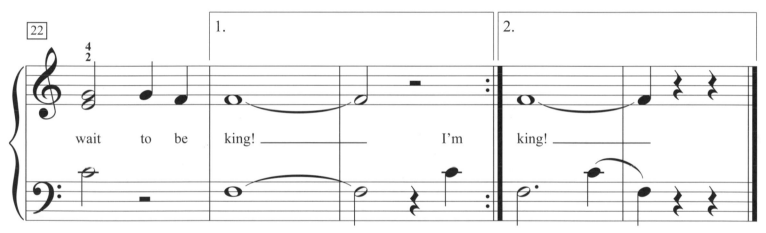

Let There Be Peace on Earth

Words and Music by Sy Miller
and Jill Jackson
Arranged by Fred Kern

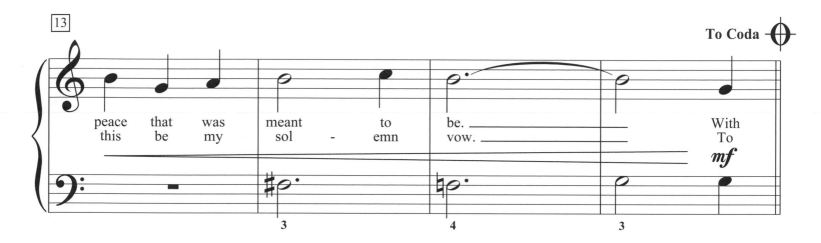

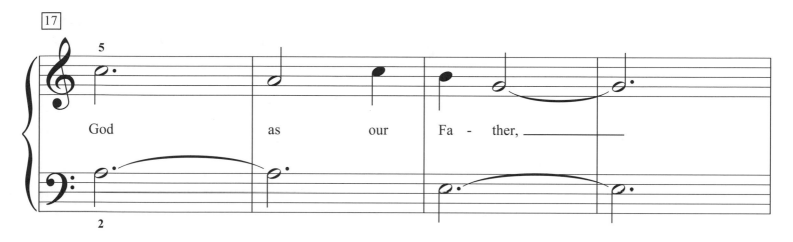

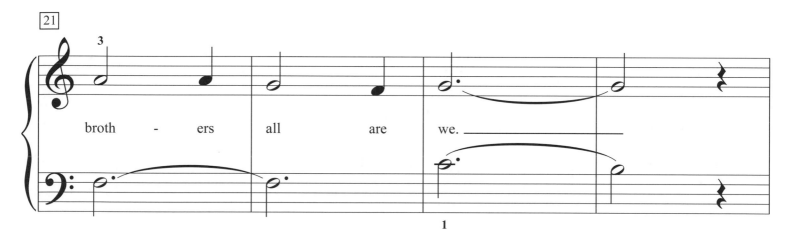

61

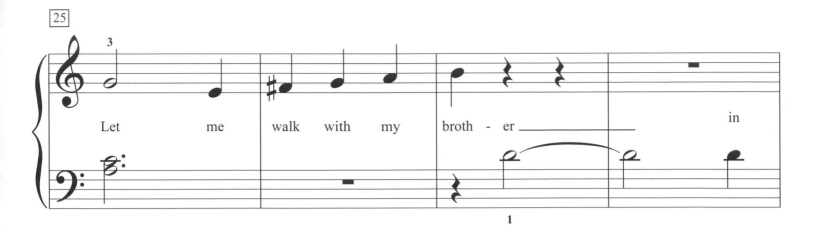

Let me walk with my broth - er _____ in

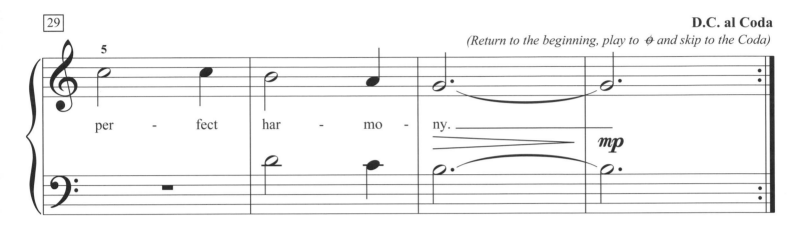

D.C. al Coda
(Return to the beginning, play to ϕ and skip to the Coda)

per - fect har - mo - ny. _____ *mp*

CODA

take each mo - ment and live each mo - ment in

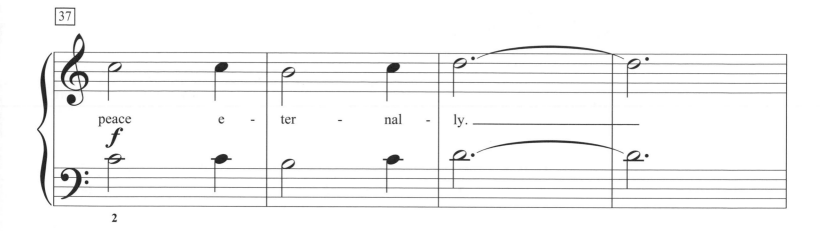

peace e - ter - nal - ly. _____

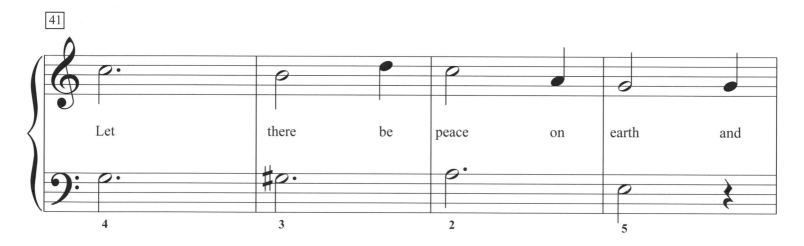

Let there be peace on earth and

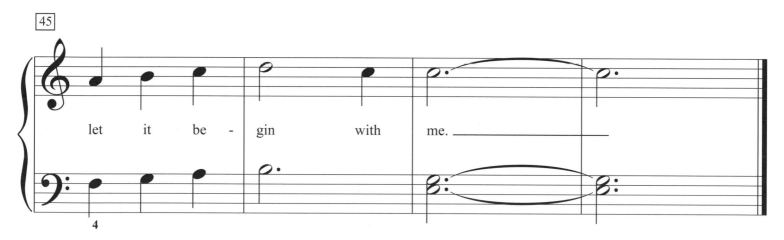

let it be - gin with me. _____

Love Changes Everything

from ASPECTS OF LOVE

Music by Andrew Lloyd Webber
Lyrics by Don Black and Charles Hart
Arranged by Carol Klose

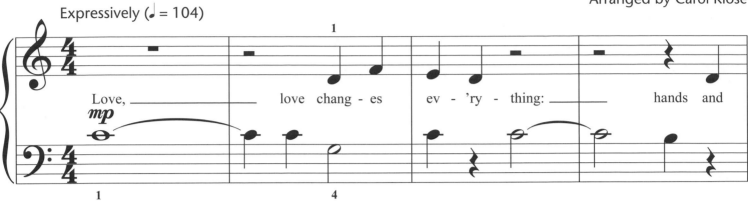

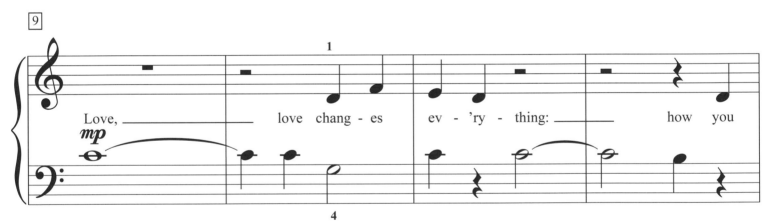

Accompaniment (Student plays one octave higher than written.)

Expressively (♩ = 104)

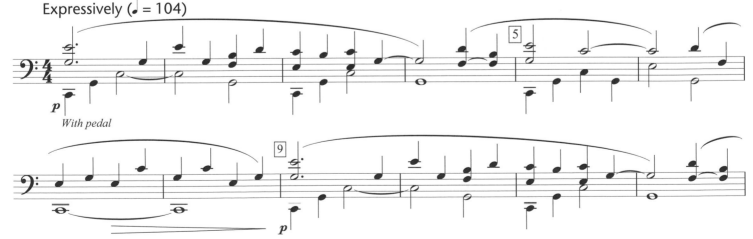

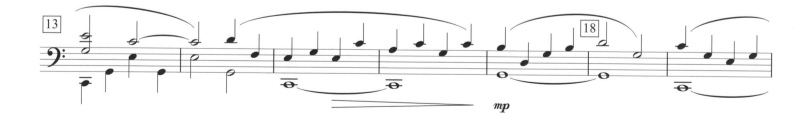

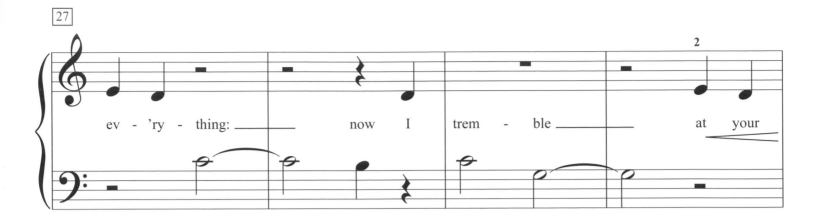

ev - 'ry - thing: _____ now I trem - ble _____ at your

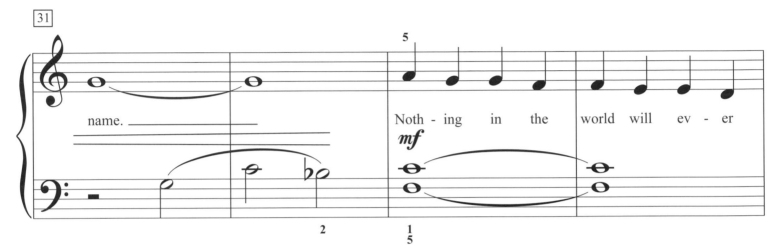

name. _____ Noth - ing in the world will ev - er

mf

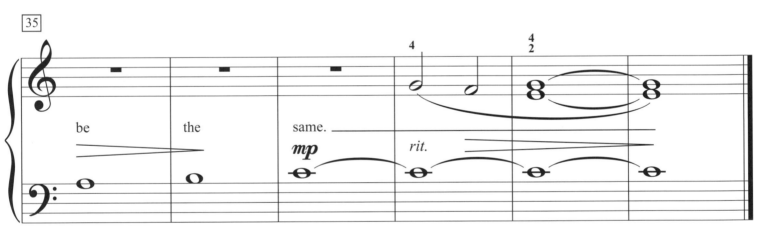

be the same. _____

mp   *rit.*

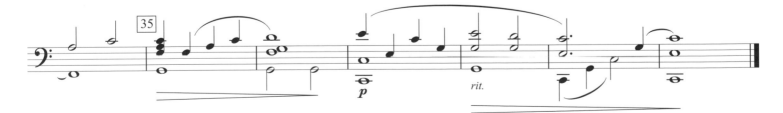

p   *rit.*

My Favorite Things

from THE SOUND OF MUSIC

Lyrics by Oscar Hammerstein II
Music by Richard Rodgers
Arranged by Fred Kern

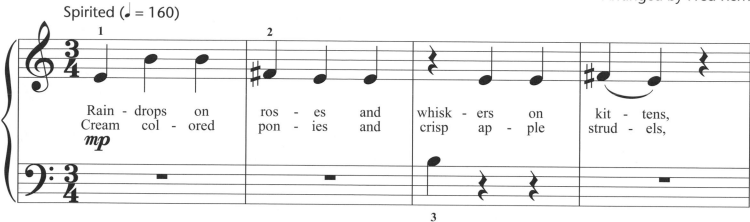

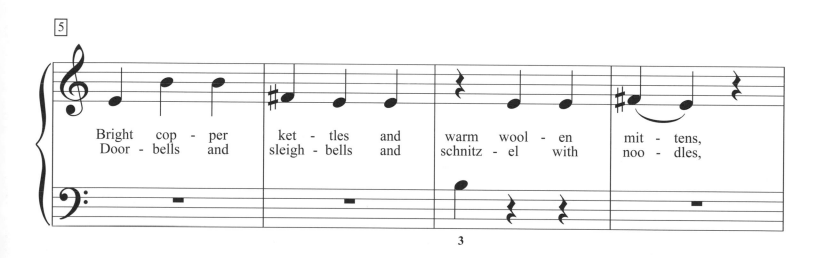

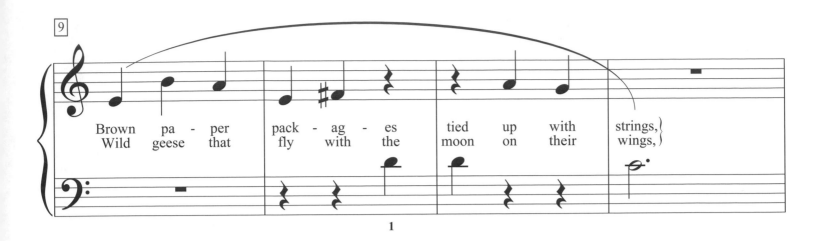

Brown pa - per pack - ag - es tied up with strings,}
Wild geese that fly with the moon on their wings,}

These are a few of my fa - vor - ite things.

When the dog bites, when the bee stings,

f

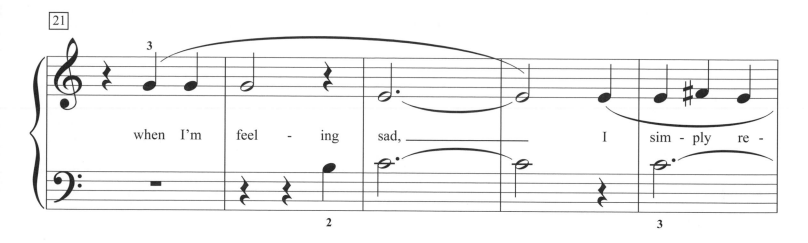

when I'm feel - ing sad, _____ I sim - ply re -

mem - ber my fa - vor - ite things, and then I don't

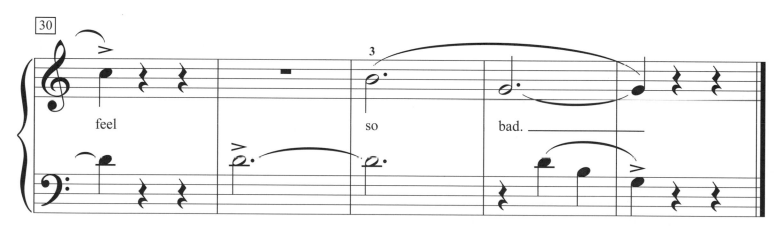

feel so bad. _____

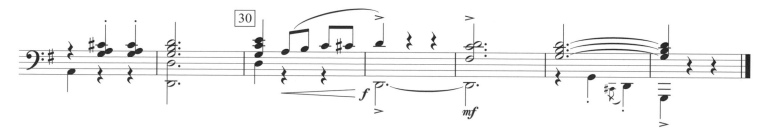

Sing

from SESAME STREET

Words and Music by
Joe Raposo
Arranged by Fred Kern

Lively, in "two" (♩ = 79)

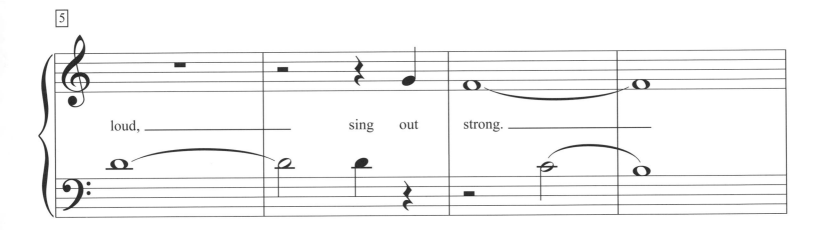

Accompaniment (Student plays one octave higher than written.)

Lively, in "two" (♩ = 79)

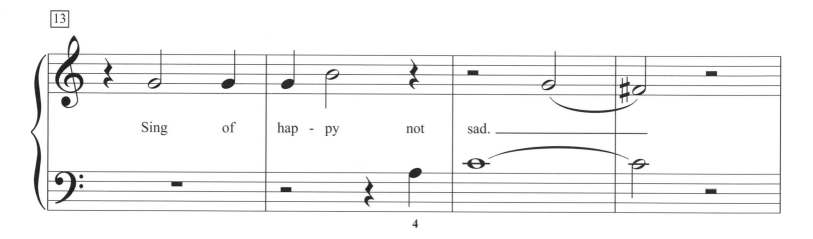

Sing of good things, not bad;

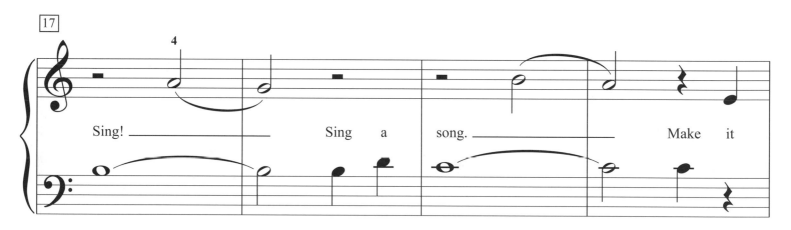

Sing of hap - py not sad.

Sing! Sing a song. Make it

sim - ple   to   last your whole life   long. _____   Don't

worry that   it's   not   good   e - nough   for   any - one else to   hear.

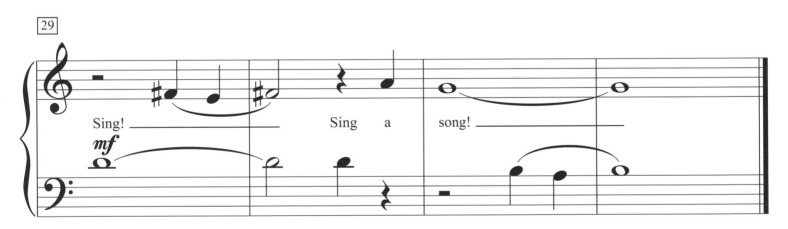

Sing! _____   Sing   a   song! _____

Somewhere Out There

from AN AMERICAN TAIL

Music by Barry Mann and James Horner
Lyric by Cynthia Weil
Arranged by Bill Boyd

Some - where out there be - neath the pale moon - light, some - one's think - ing of me and lov - ing me to - night. Some - where

Accompaniment (Student plays one octave higher than written.)

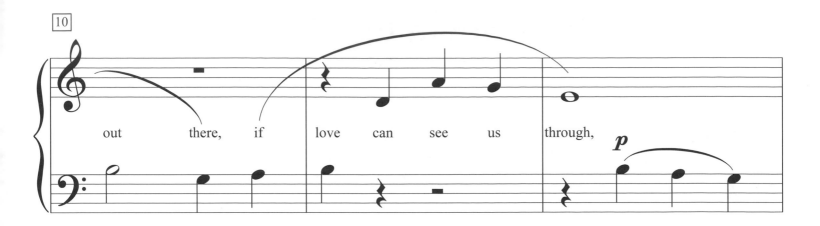

out there, if love can see us through, *p*

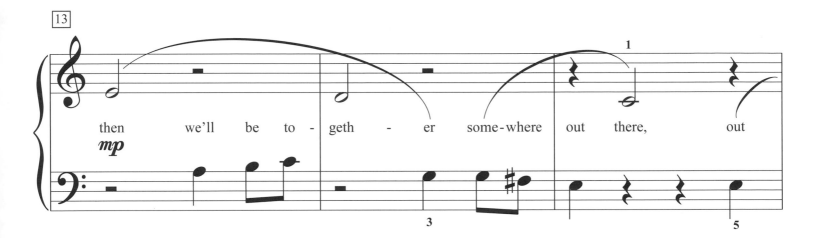

then we'll be to - geth - er some-where out there, out

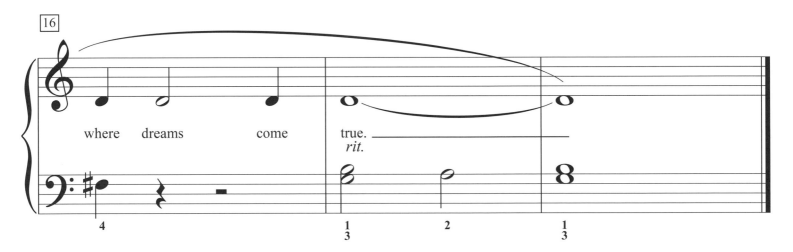

where dreams come true. ___ *rit.*

74

When She Loved Me

from TOY STORY 2

Music and Lyrics by
Randy Newman
Arranged by Mona Rejino

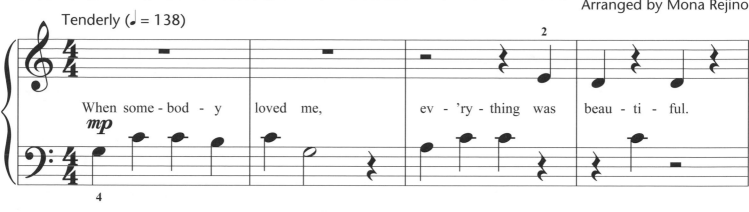

When some-bod-y loved me, ev-'ry-thing was beau-ti-ful.

Ev-'ry hour we spent to-geth-er lives with-in my heart.

And when she was sad, I was there to dry her tears;

Accompaniment (Student plays one octave higher than written.)

and when she was hap - py, so was I, when she loved

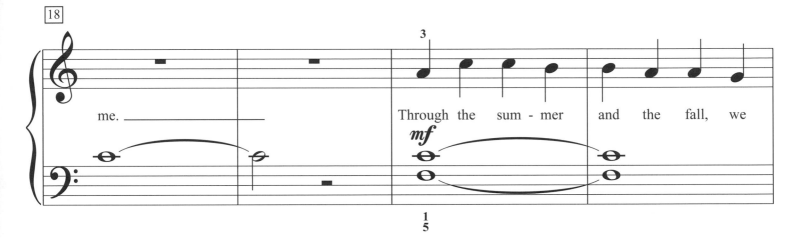

me. _____ Through the sum - mer and the fall, we

had each oth - er, that was all. Just she and I to - geth - er, like

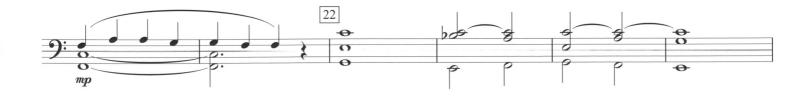

it was meant to be. And when she was lone - ly,

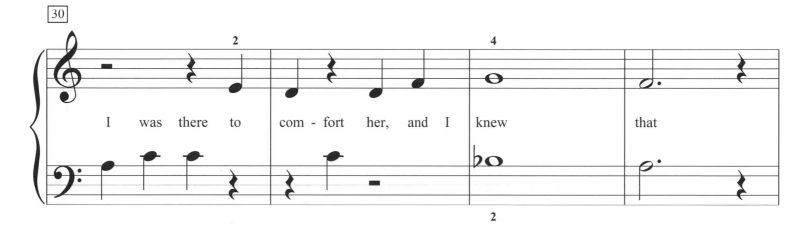

I was there to com - fort her, and I knew that

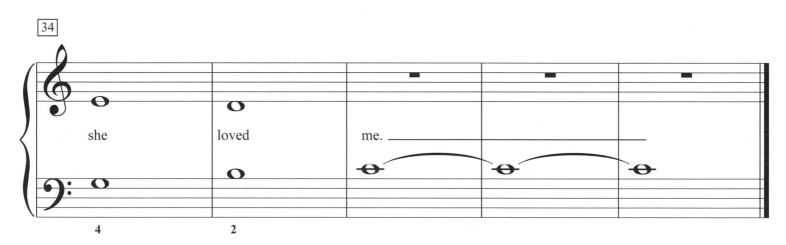

she loved me. _____

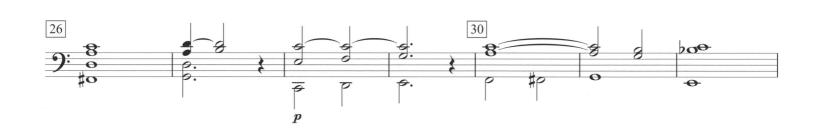

You'll Be in My Heart

from TARZAN™

Words and Music by
Phil Collins
Arranged by Mona Rejino

Moderately fast, with expression (♩ = 92)

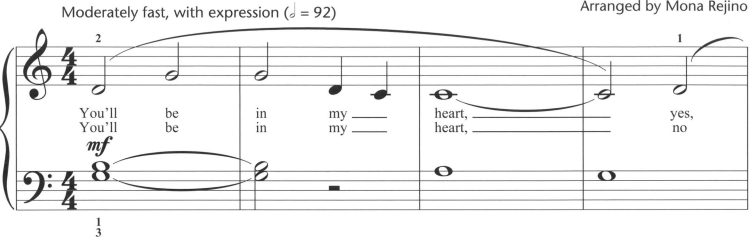

You'll be in my ____ heart, _____ yes,
You'll be in my ____ heart, _____ no

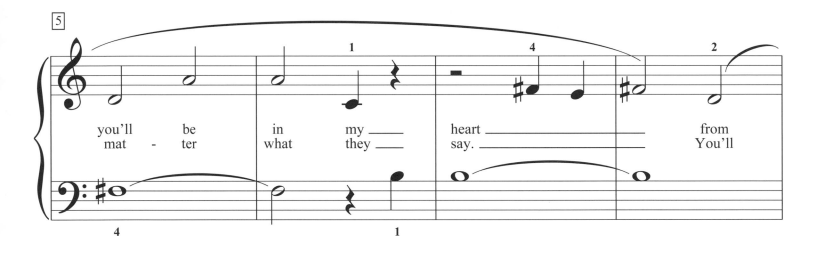

you'll be in my ____ heart _____ from
mat - ter in what they ____ say. _____ You'll

Accompaniment (Student plays one octave higher than written.)

Moderately fast, with expression (♩ = 92)

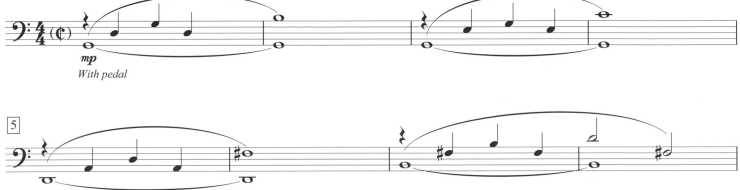

mp
With pedal

this day on now and for - ev - er -
be here in my heart _____ al -

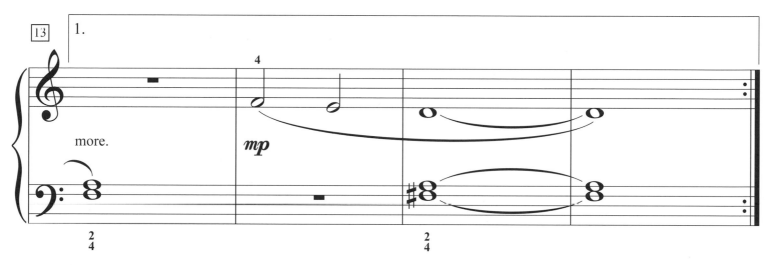

1.
more. *mp*

2.
ways. I'll be there al - ways.
rit.

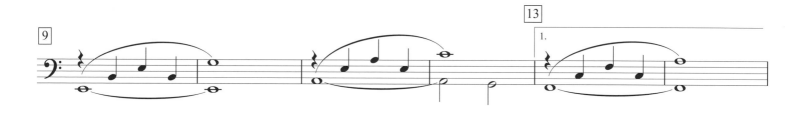

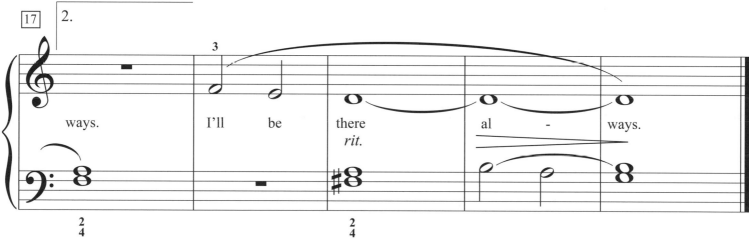
p

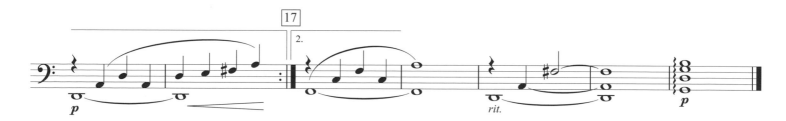
p   *rit.*   *p*

Zip-A-Dee-Doo-Dah
from SONG OF THE SOUTH

Words by Ray Gilbert
Music by Allie Wrubel
Arranged by Mona Rejino

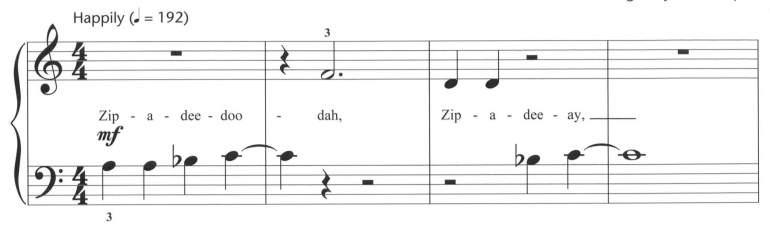

Zip - a - dee - doo - dah, Zip - a - dee - ay, ___

My, oh my, ___ what a won - der - ful day! ___

Accompaniment (Student plays one octave higher than written.)

Plen - ty of sun - shine, head - in' my way,

Zip - a - dee - doo - dah, Zip - a - dee - ay! _____ Mis - ter
mp

Blue - bird on my shoul - der, _____ It's the
mf

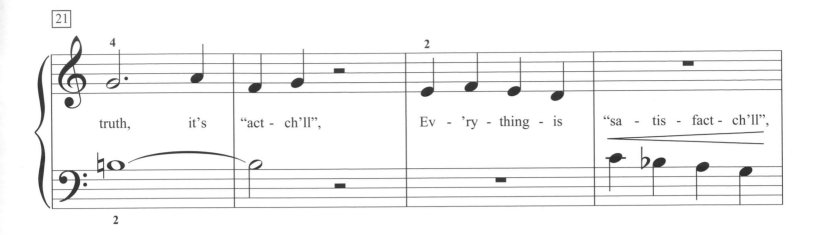

America, the Beautiful

Words by Katherine Lee Bates
Music by Samuel A. Ward
Arranged by Phillip Keveren

Moderately, deeply expressive (♩ = 90)

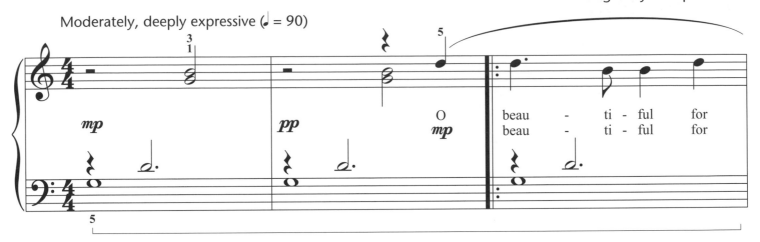

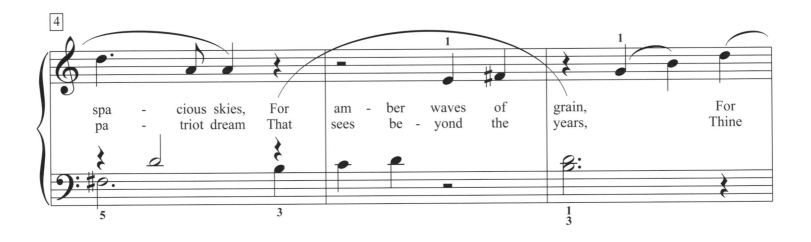

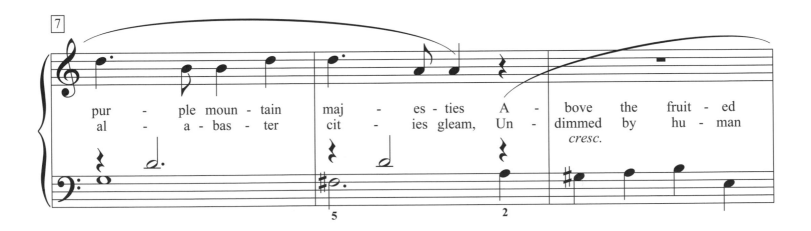

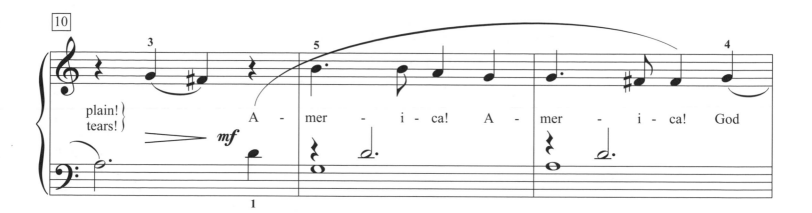

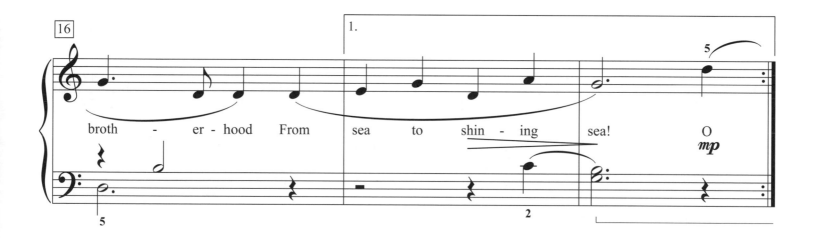

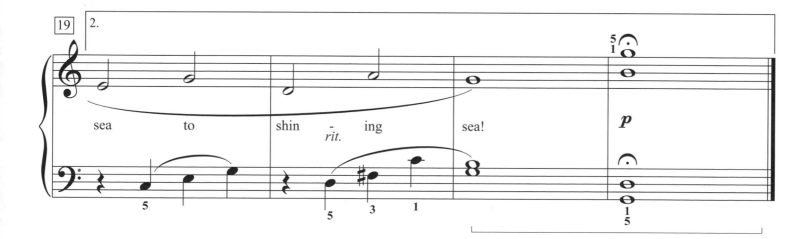

85

Be Our Guest

from BEAUTY AND THE BEAST

Music by Alan Menken
Lyrics by Howard Ashman
Arranged by Mona Rejino

With spirit, in "two" (♩ = 100)

Be our guest! Be our guest! Put our ser- vice to the

test. Tie your nap - kin 'round your neck, *che - rie,* and we pro - vide the

Accompaniment (Student plays one octave higher than written.)

With spirit, in "two" (♩ = 100)

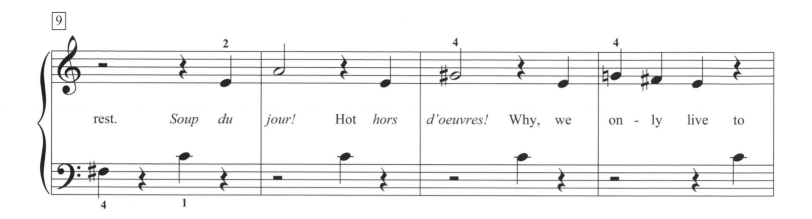

rest. *Soup du jour!* Hot *hors d'oeuvres!* Why, we on - ly live to

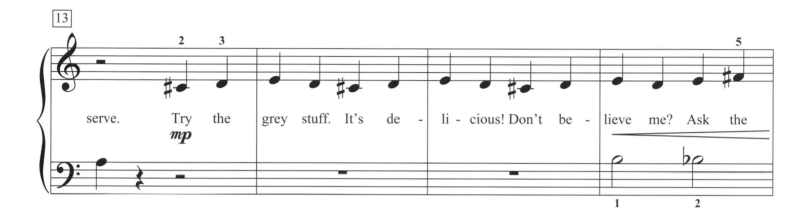

serve. Try the grey stuff. It's de - li - cious! Don't be - lieve me? Ask the

mp

dish - es! They can sing! They can dance! Af - ter all, Miss, this is

mf

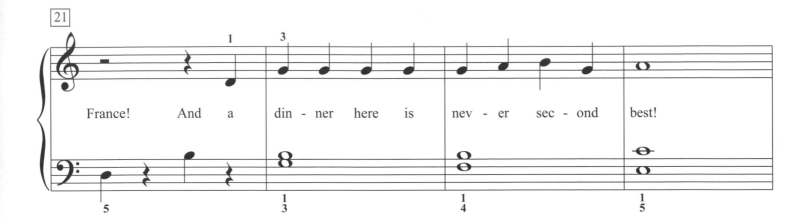

France! And a din - ner here is nev - er sec - ond best!

Go on, un - fold your men - u. Take a glance and then __

f

__ you'll be our guest! Be our guest! Be our guest!

mf

A Dream Is a Wish Your Heart Makes

from CINDERELLA

Words and Music by Mack David,
Al Hoffman and Jerry Livingston
Arranged by Phillip Keveren

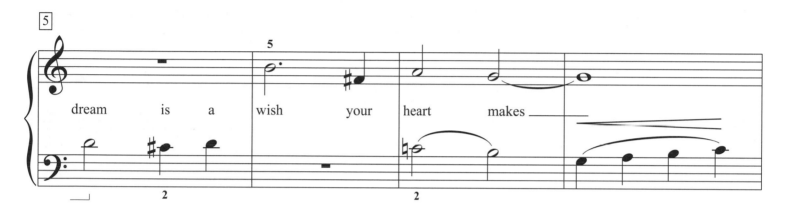

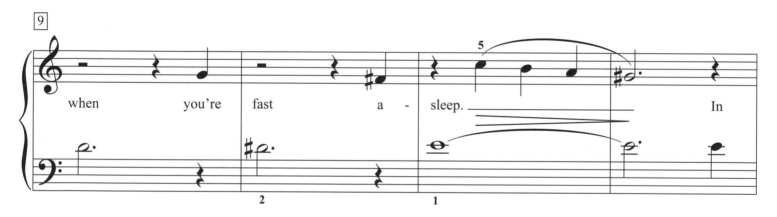

Accompaniment (Student plays one octave higher than written.)

With tenderness, in 'two' (♩ = 72)

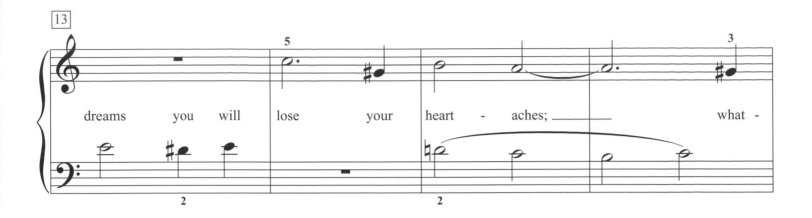

dreams you will lose your heart - aches; _____ what -

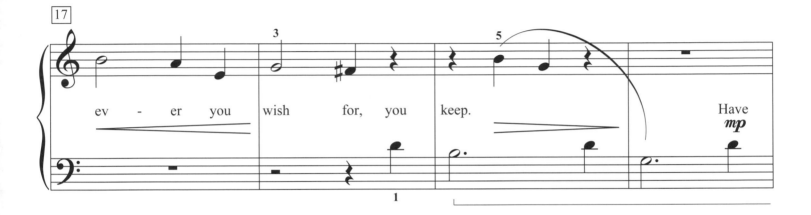

ev - er you wish for, you keep. Have

mp

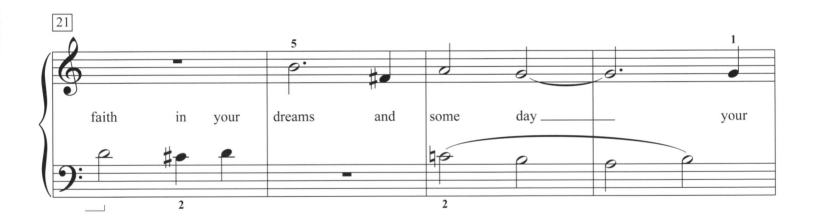

faith in your dreams and some day _____ your

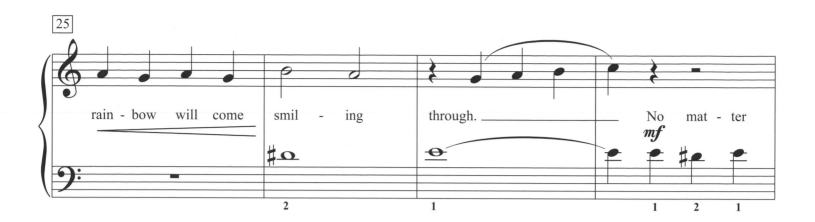

Do You Want to Build a Snowman?

from FROZEN

Music and Lyrics by Kristen Anderson-Lopez
and Robert Lopez
Arranged by Jennifer Linn

Moderately fast (♩ = 144)

With pedal

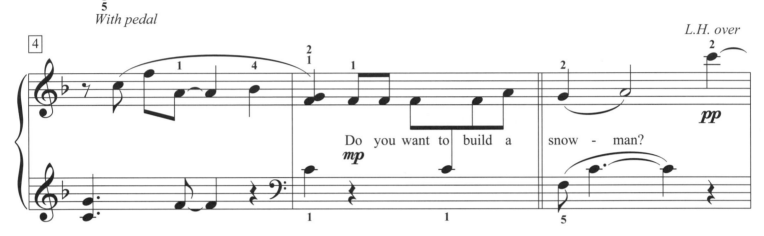

Do you want to build a snow-man?

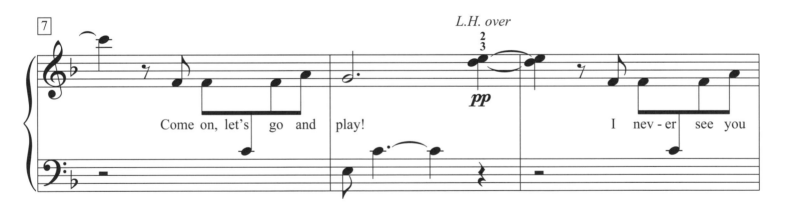

Come on, let's go and play! I nev-er see you

an-y-more. Come out the door! It's like you've gone a-way.

We used to be best bud - dies, but now we're not. ___ I

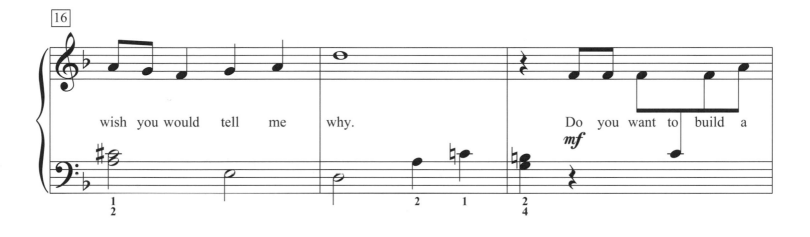

wish you would tell me why. Do you want to build a

snow - man? It does-n't have to be a snow - man.

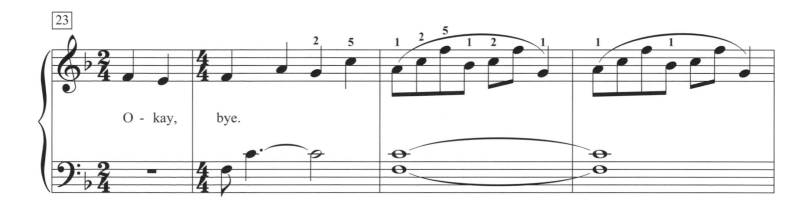

O - kay, bye.

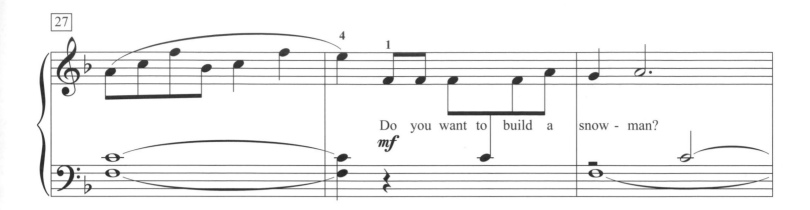

Do you want to build a snow-man?

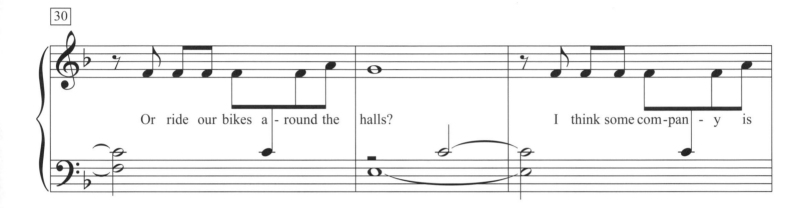

Or ride our bikes a-round the halls? I think some com-pan - y is

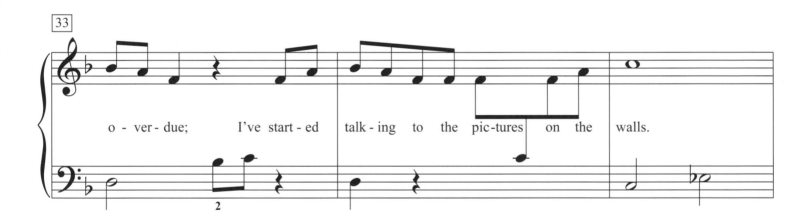

o - ver-due; I've start-ed talk-ing to the pic-tures on the walls.

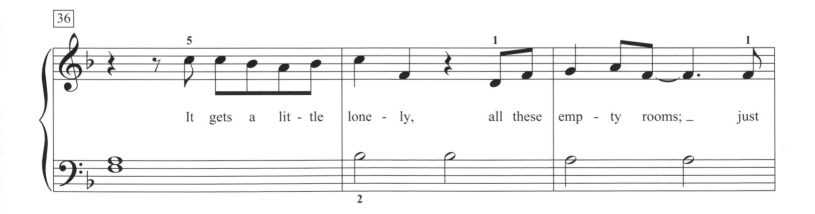

It gets a lit-tle lone-ly, all these emp-ty rooms; just

watch - ing the hours tick by.

Make "click-clock" sound with tongue

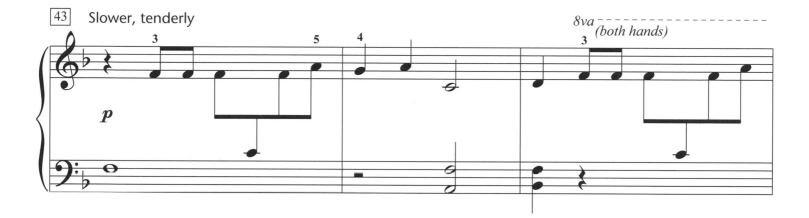

43 Slower, tenderly

8va - - - - - - - - - - - - - - -
(both hands)

p

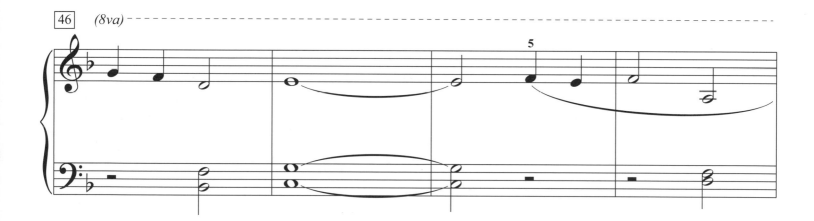

46 *(8va)* -

Very slowly

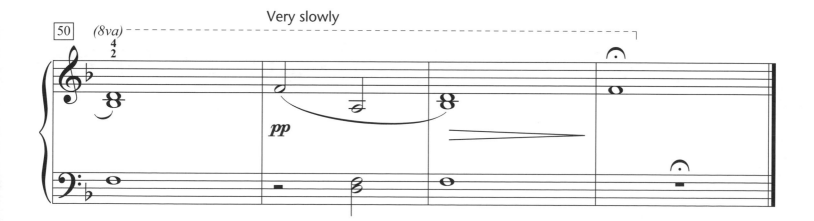

50 *(8va)* -

pp

Firework

Words and Music by Katy Perry,
Mikkel Eriksen, Tor Erik Hermansen,
Esther Dean and Sandy Wilhelm
Arranged by Mona Rejino

Moderately fast (♩ = 120)

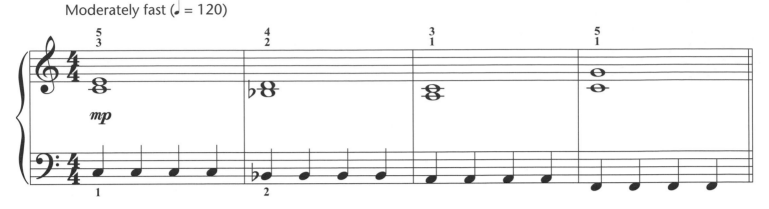

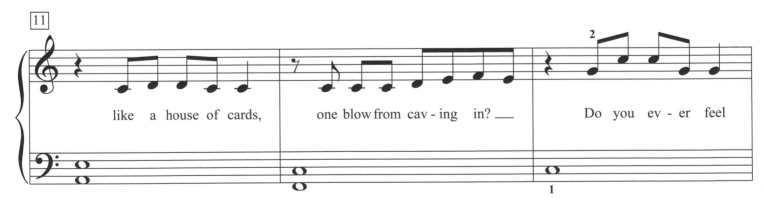

al - read - y bur - ied deep, six feet un - der screams, but no one seems to hear a thing?

Do you know that there's still a chance for you? 'Cause there's a spark in you.

You just got - ta ig - nite ___ the light ___ and let ___

___ it shine. ___ Just own ___ the night ___

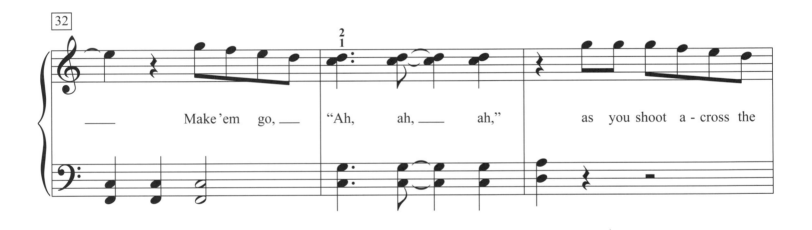

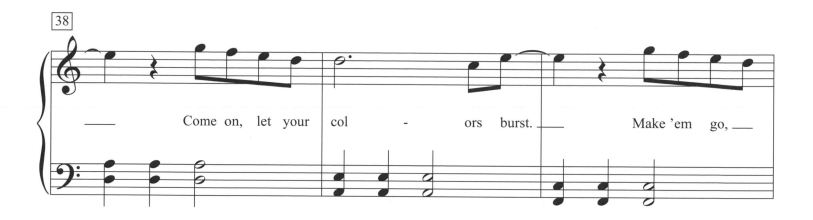

Come on, let your col - ors burst. Make 'em go,

"Ah, ah, ah." You're gon - na leave 'em all in awe, awe, awe.

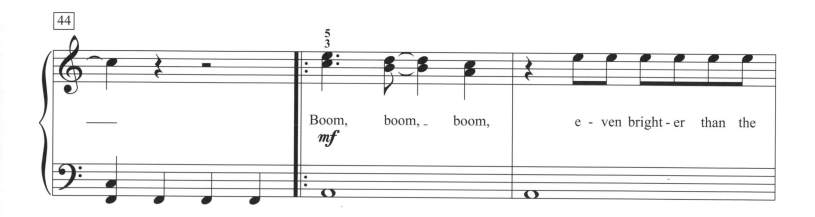

Boom, boom, boom, *mf* e - ven bright - er than the

moon, moon, moon.

God Help the Outcasts

from THE HUNCHBACK OF NOTRE DAME

Music by Alan Menken
Lyrics by Stephen Schwartz
Arranged by Phillip Keveren

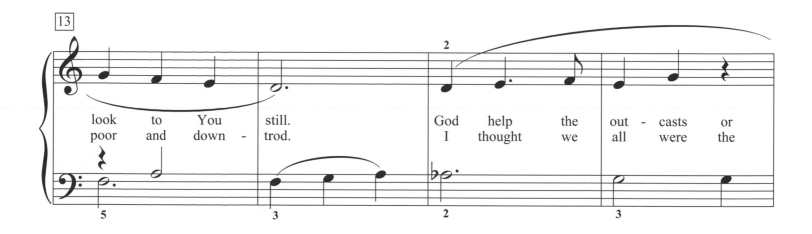

look to You still.
poor and down - trod.

God help the out - casts or
I thought we all were the

no - bod - y will.
chil - dren of

will.

p

God. _____

God help the out - casts,

rit.

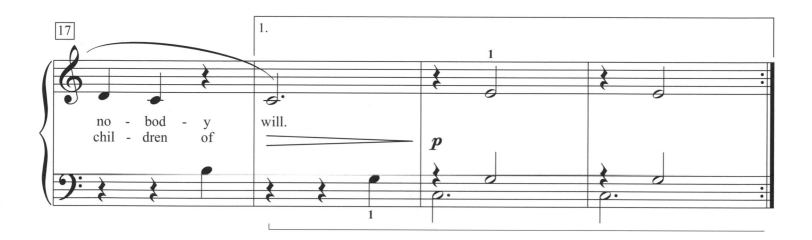

chil - dren of God.

p   *a tempo*

rit.

pp

101

Hello

Words and Music by Adele Adkins
and Greg Kurstin
Arranged by Jennifer Linn

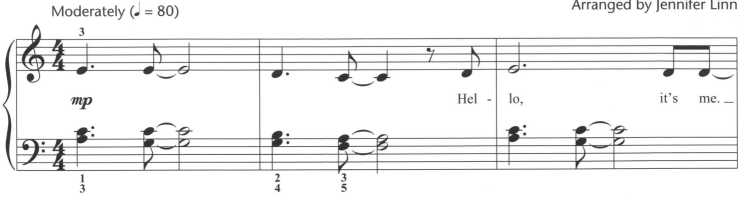

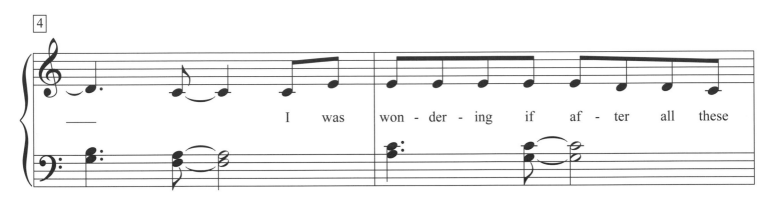

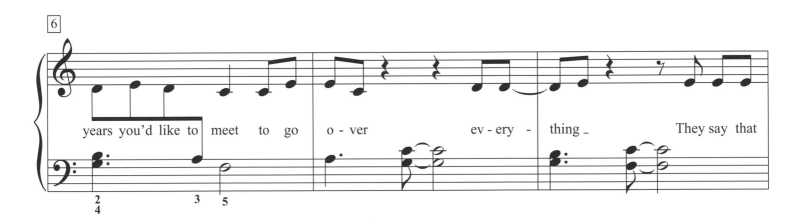

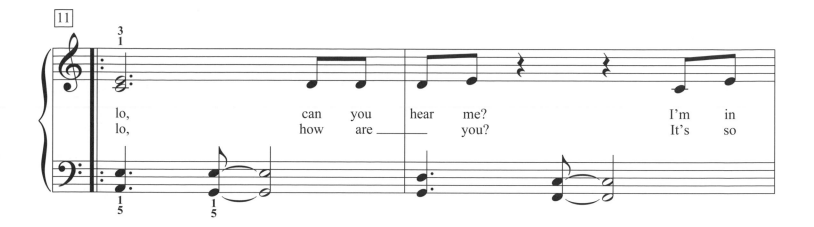

11

lo,   can   you   hear   me?   I'm   in
lo,   how   are   you?   It's   so

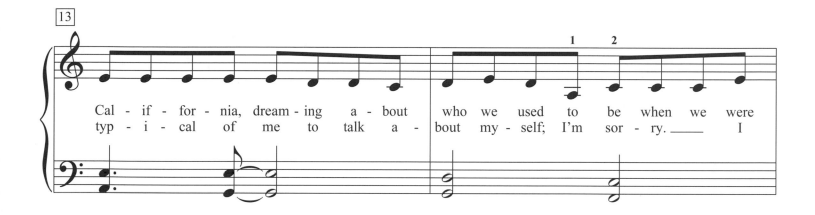

13

Cal - if - for - nia, dream - ing   a - bout   who   we   used   to   be   when   we   were
typ - i - cal   of   me   to   talk   a - bout   my - self;   I'm   sor - ry.   I

15

young - er   and   free.   I've   for -
hope   that   you're   well.   Did   you

17

got - ten   how   it   felt   be - fore   the   world   fell   at   our   feet. There's   such   a
ev - er   make   it   out   of   that   town   where   noth - ing   ev - er   hap - pened?   It's   no

dif - f'rence ____ be - tween ____ us, ____ and a mil - li - on ____ miles. ____
se - cret ____ that both of us ____ are run - ning out of time. ____

Hel - lo from the oth - er side. ____ I

must have called a thou-sand times ____ to tell you ____ I'm sor - ry for every-

thing that I've done, ____ but when I call, you ____ nev - er seem to be home. ____

Hel - lo from the out - side. _____ At least I can say that I've tried _____

_____ to tell you _____ I'm sor - ry for break - in' your heart. But it don't mat -

To Coda ⊕

ter: it clear - ly doesn't tear you a - part an - y - more. _____

Hel - tear you a - part _____ an - y - more _____

105

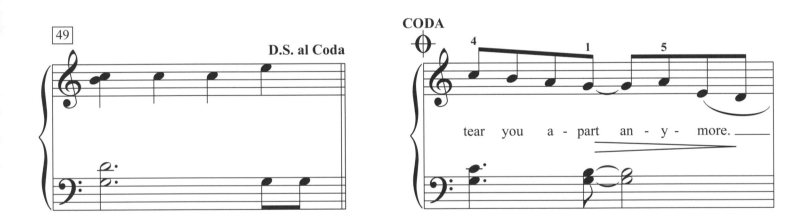

D.S. al Coda

CODA

tear you a - part an - y - more.

mp

Little Shop of Horrors

from the Stage Production LITTLE SHOP OF HORRORS

Words by Howard Ashman
Music by Alan Menken
Arranged by Fred Kern

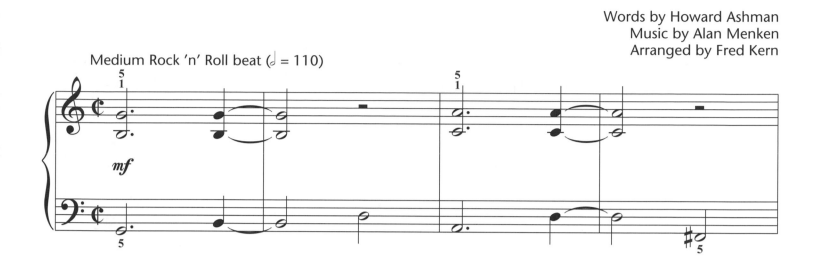

Lit - tle shop, ___ lit - tle shop - pa hor - rors.
Lit - tle shop, ___ lit - tle shop - pa hor - rors.
Lit - tle shop, ___ lit - tle shop - pa hor - rors.

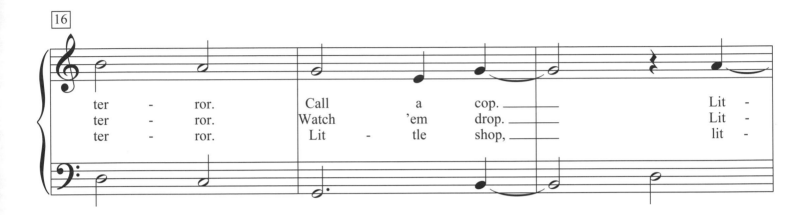

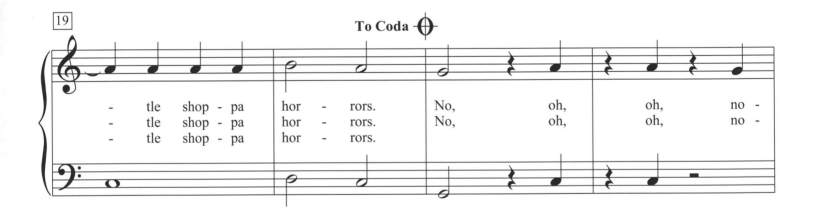

what a creep - y thing to be hap - pen - ing! _____ (Look

out, look out, look out, look out!) *mf* Shang - a - lang, feel

_____ the sturm and drang in the air. _____

(Yeah, __ yeah, __ yeah.) *f* Sha - la - la,

stop right where you are. Don't move a thing. ___

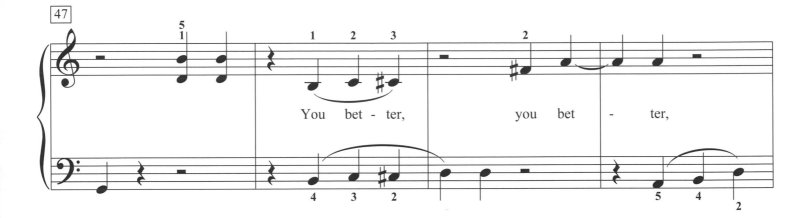

You bet - ter, you bet - ter,

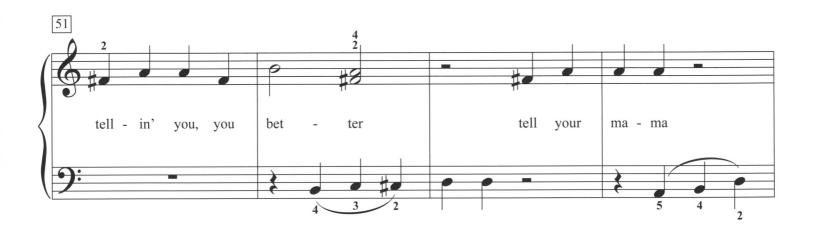

tell - in' you, you bet - ter tell your ma - ma

some - thin's gon - na get her. *mp* She bet - ter,

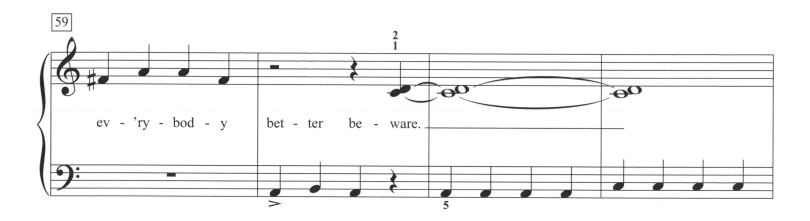

ev - 'ry - bod - y   bet - ter   be - ware.

D.S. al Coda

(Com - ma,   com - ma,   com - ma)

CODA

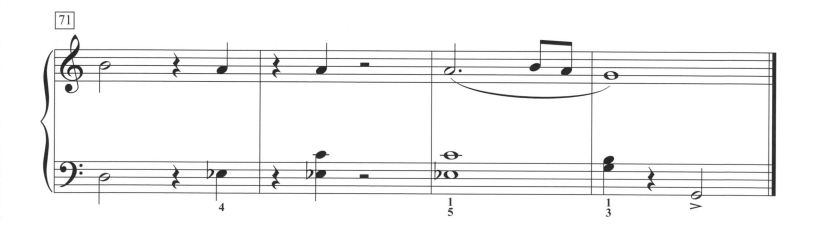

I Whistle a Happy Tune

from THE KING AND I

Lyrics by Oscar Hammerstein II
Music by Richard Rodgers
Arranged by Fred Kern

Moderately, in 'two' (♩ = 84)

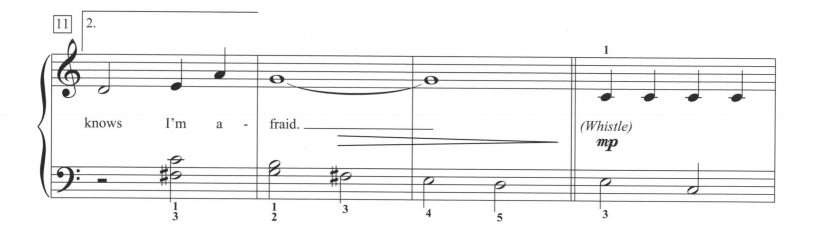

knows I'm a- fraid. _____ (Whistle)

You may be as

brave as you make be - lieve you

are. _____

The Music of the Night
from THE PHANTOM OF THE OPERA

Music by Andrew Lloyd Webber
Lyrics by Charles Hart
Additional Lyrics by Richard Stilgoe
Arranged by Mona Rejino

Slowly (♩ = 69)

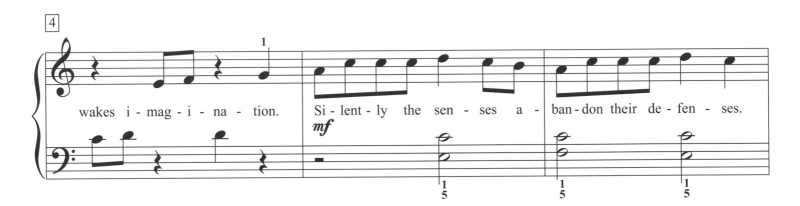

Night time sharp - ens, height-ens each sen-sa - tion; dark - ness stirs and

mp legato

wakes i - mag - i - na - tion. Si - lent-ly the sen - ses a - ban-don their de-fen - ses.

mf

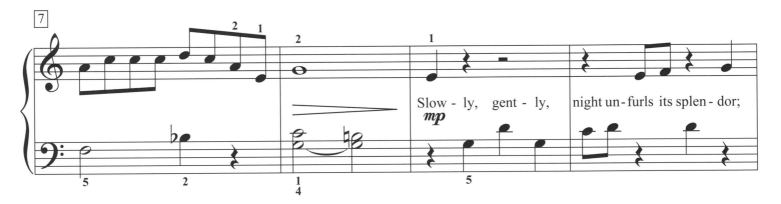

Slow - ly, gent - ly, night un-furls its splen - dor;

mp

Accompaniment (Student plays one octave higher than written.)

Slowly (♩ = 69)

p

With pedal

mp

p

grasp it, sense it, trem - u - lous and ten - der. Turn your face a - way from the

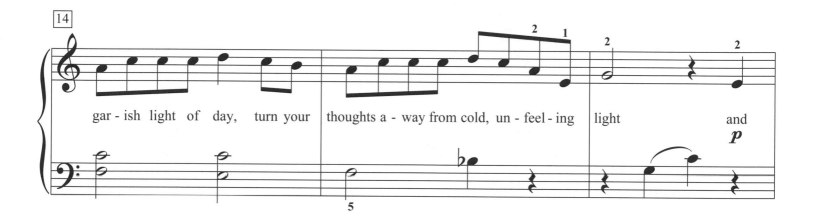

gar - ish light of day, turn your thoughts a - way from cold, un - feel - ing light and

lis - ten to the mu - sic of the night. _____

115

Once Upon a Dream

from SLEEPING BEAUTY

Words and Music by Sammy Fain
and Jack Lawrence
Adapted from a Theme by Tchaikovsky
Arranged by Fred Kern

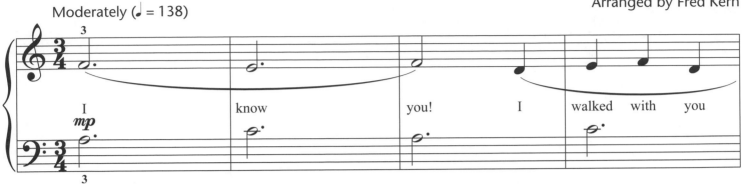

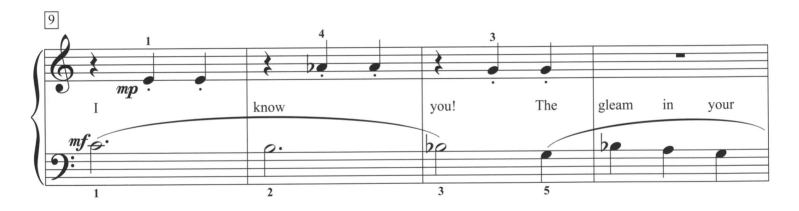

Accompaniment (Student plays one octave higher than written.)

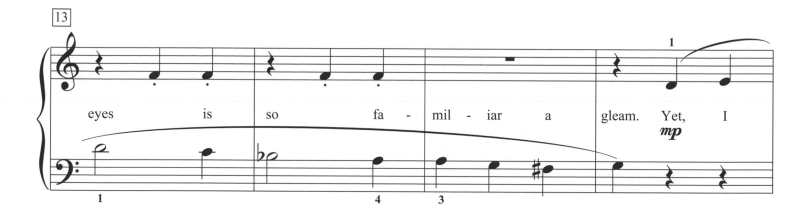

eyes is so fa - mil - iar a gleam. Yet, I

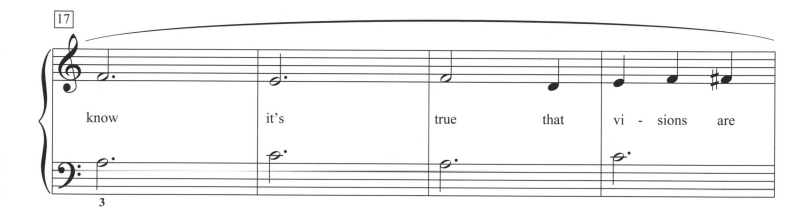

know it's true that vi - sions are

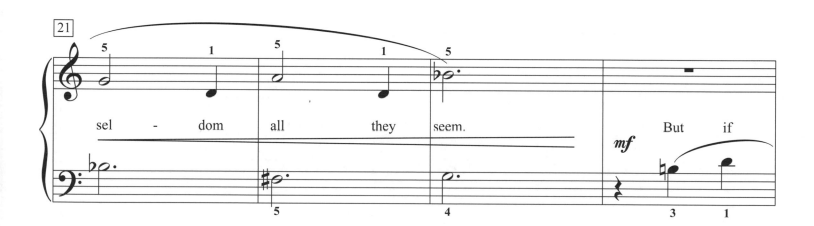

sel - dom all they seem. But if

I know you, I know what you'll do ____

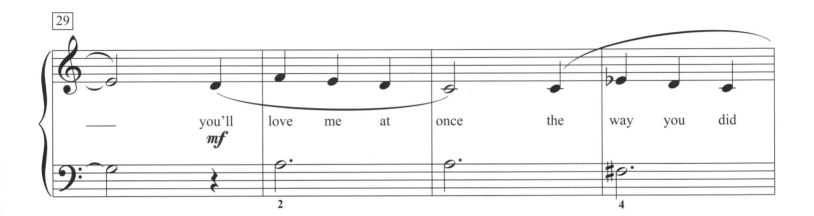

____ you'll love me at once the way you did

once up - on a dream. ____

118

The Rainbow Connection

from THE MUPPET MOVIE

Words and Music by Paul Williams
and Kenneth L. Ascher
Arranged by Fred Kern

Moderately, with a lilt; swing eighth notes (♩ = 92)

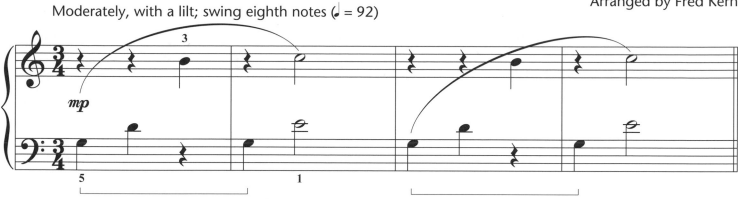

Why are there so man - y songs a - bout
Who said that ev - 'ry wish would be heard and

rain - bows, and what's on the oth - er side? _____
an - swered when wished on the morn - ing star? _____

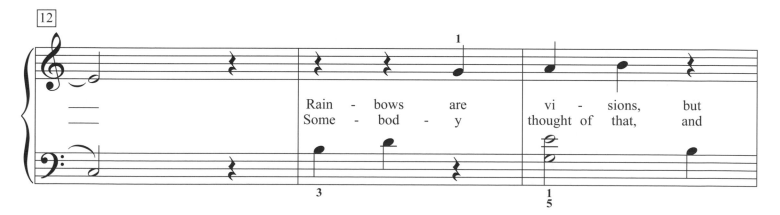

_____ Rain - bows are vi - sions, but
_____ Some - bod - y thought of that, and

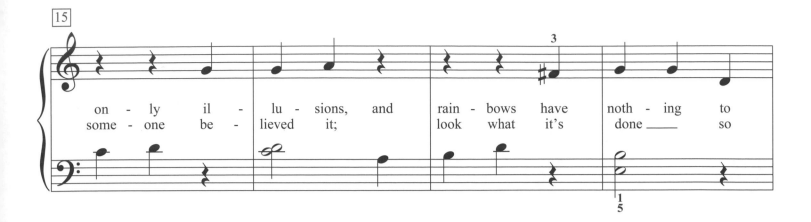

on - ly il - lu - sions, and rain - bows have noth - ing to
some - one be - lieved it; look what it's done _____ so

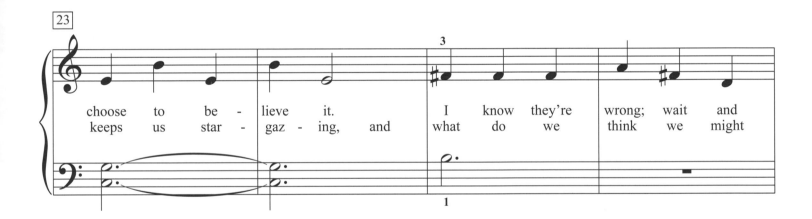

hide. _____ So we've been told, and some
far. _____ What's so a - maz - ing that

choose to be - lieve it. I know they're wrong; wait and
keeps us star - gaz - ing, and what do we think we might

see. _____ Some - day we'll find it, the
see? _____ *mp* *mf*

120

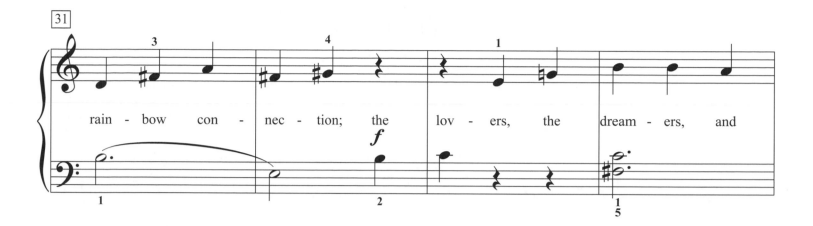

rain - bow con - nec - tion; the *f* lov - ers, the dream - ers, and

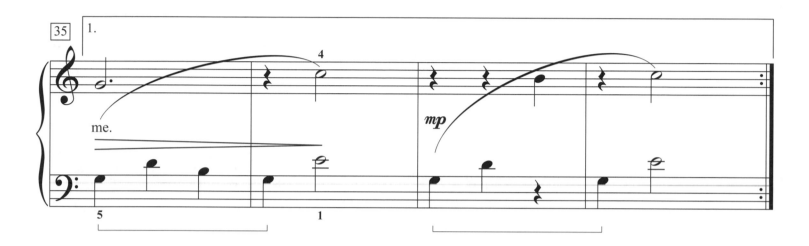

1.
me. *mp*

2.
me. La da da dee da da do la

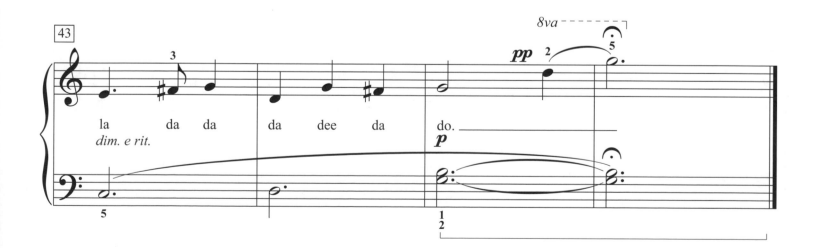

la da da da dee da do.
dim. e rit. *p*

Part of Your World

from THE LITTLE MERMAID

Music by Alan Menken
Lyrics by Howard Ashman
Arranged by Mona Rejino

Moderately bright (♩ = 112)

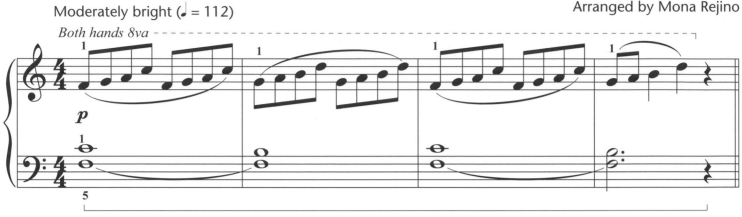

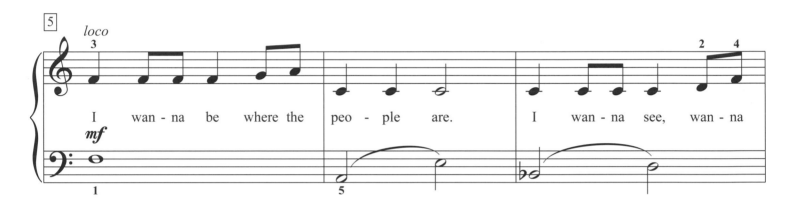

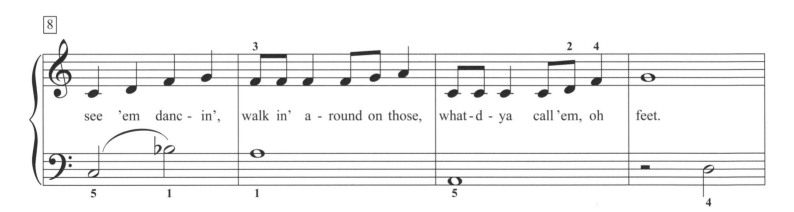

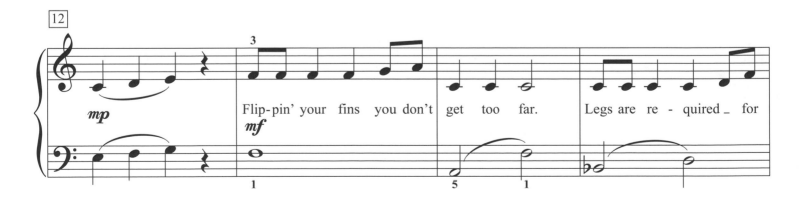

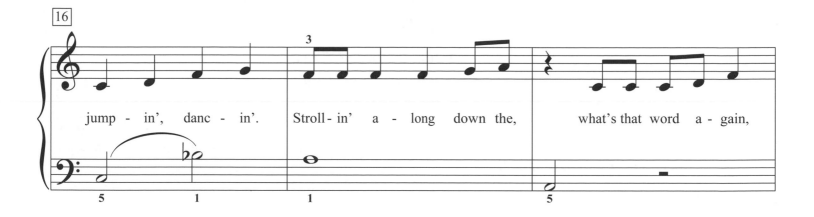

jump - in', danc - in'. Stroll - in' a - long down the, what's that word a - gain,

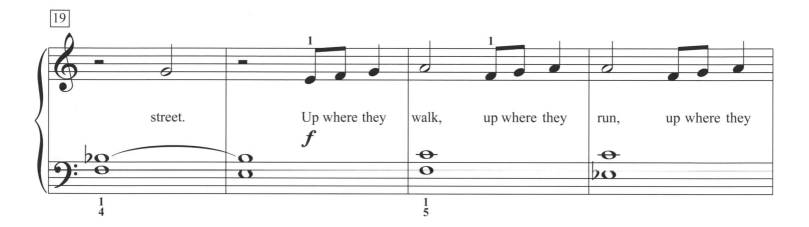

street. Up where they walk, up where they run, up where they

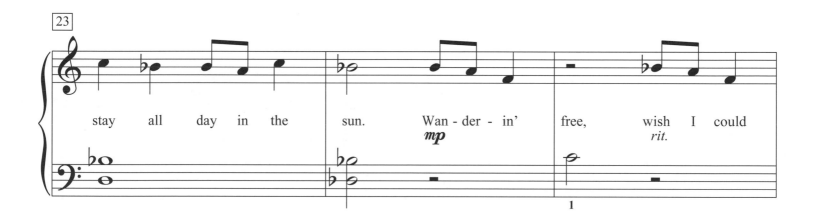

stay all day in the sun. Wan - der - in' free, wish I could

be part of that world.

Skyfall
from the Motion Picture SKYFALL

Words and Music by Adele Adkins
and Paul Epworth
Arranged by Mona Rejino

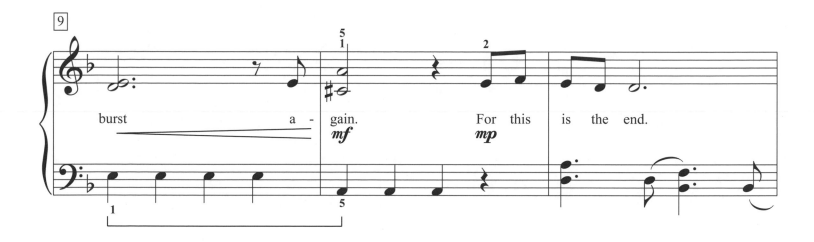

burst   a - gain.   For this   is   the end.

mf   *mp*

I've drowned and dreamt this   mo -   ment.

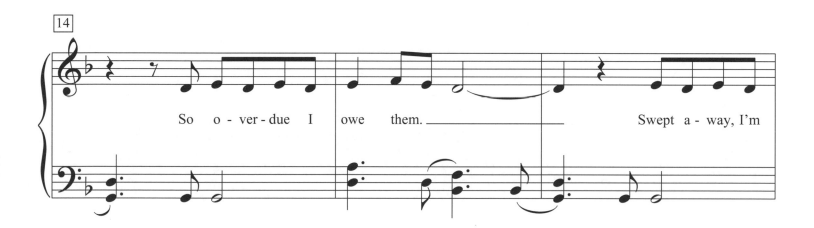

So   o - ver - due I   owe   them.   Swept a - way, I'm

stol   -   en.   Let the   sky   fall.   When it

mf

crum - bles, _____ we will stand tall, _____ face it

all to - geth - er. Let the sky fall. _____ When it crum - bles, _____ we will

stand tall, _____ face it all to - geth - er at sky - fall.

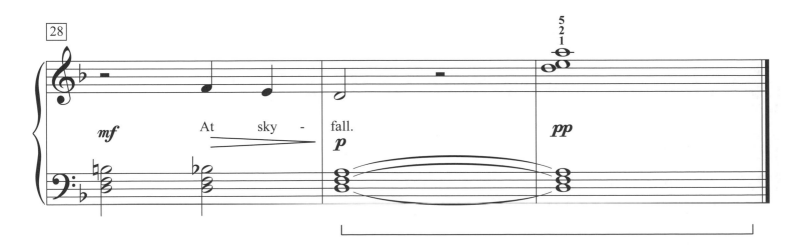

mf At sky - fall. p pp

Tomorrow

from the Musical Production ANNIE

Lyric by Martin Charnin
Music by Charles Strouse
Arranged by Mona Rejino

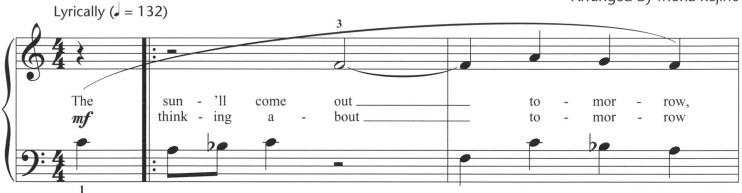

The sun - 'll come out _____ to - mor - row,
think - ing a - bout _____ to - mor - row

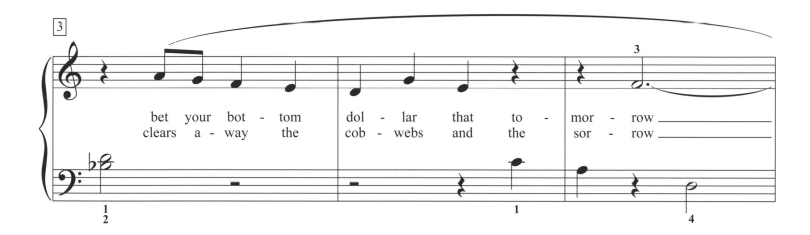

bet your bot - tom dol - lar that to - mor - row _____
clears a - way the cob - webs and the sor - row _____

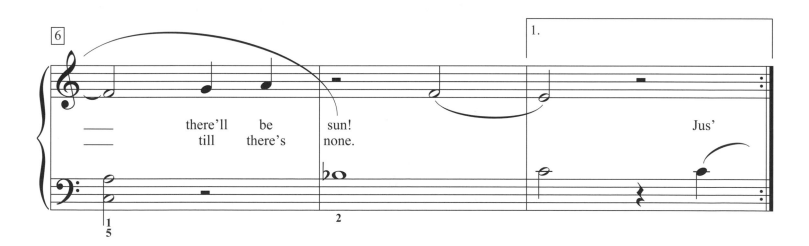

_____ there'll be sun!
_____ till there's none.

1.

Jus'

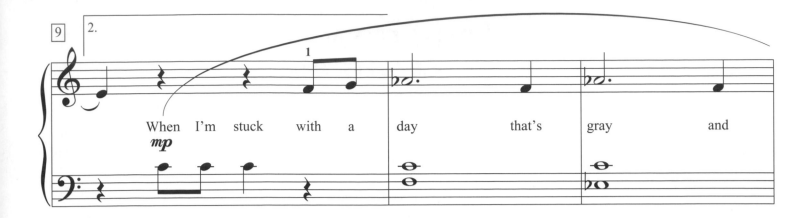

When I'm stuck with a day that's gray and

mp

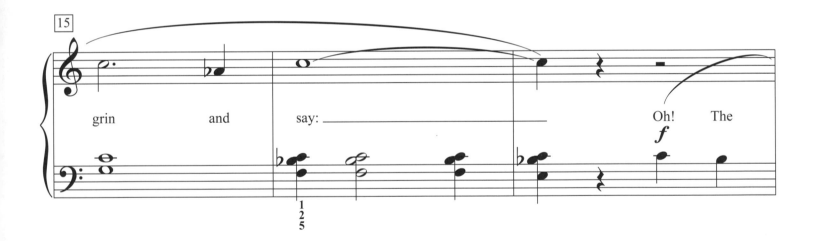

lone - ly, I just stick out my chin and

cresc.

grin and say: Oh! The

f

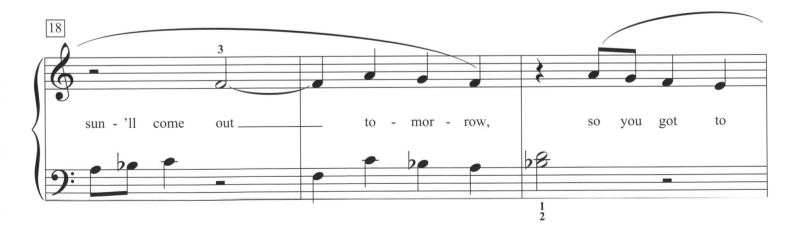

sun - 'll come out to - mor - row, so you got to

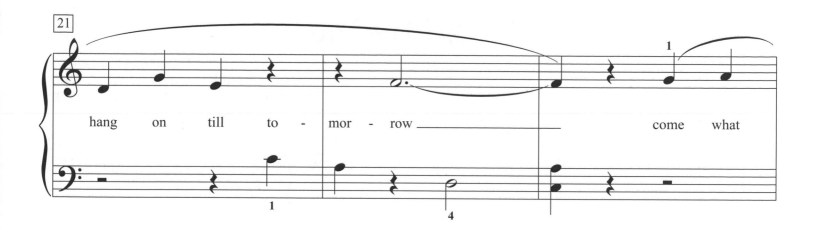

hang on till to - mor - row _____ come what

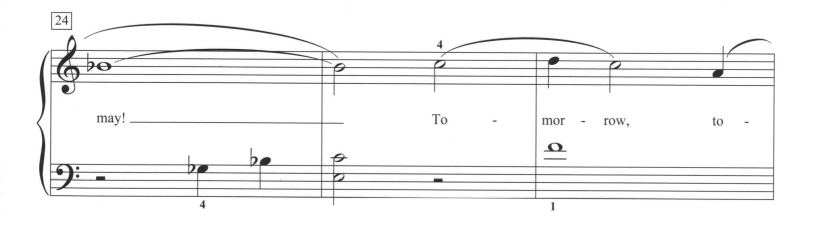

may! _____ To - mor - row, to -

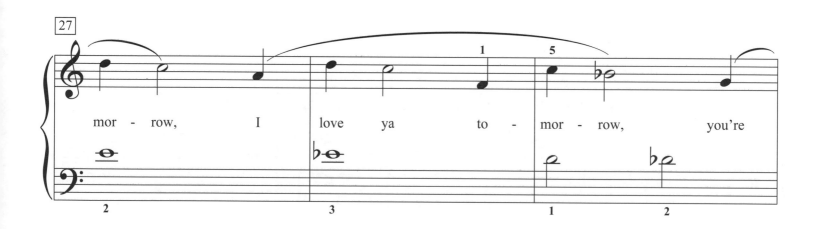

mor - row, I love ya to - mor - row, you're

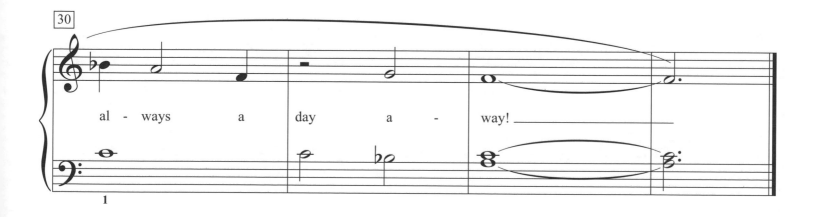

al - ways a day a - way! _____

Stand by Me

Words and Music by Jerry Leiber,
Mike Stoller and Ben E. King
Arranged by Phillip Keveren

Steady Rock beat (♩ = 100)

won't   be   a - fraid,   just   as   long _____ as you

won't   shed   a   tear,   just   as   long _____ as you

stand,   stand by   me.}

stand,   stand by   me.}   So,   dar - ling, dar - ling,

stand   by   me,   stand   by   me,   oh,

mf

1.

stand, _____   stand by me.   If the

mp

2.

me. _____   *rit.*

mp

Unchained Melody

from the Motion Picture UNCHAINED

Lyric by Hy Zaret
Music by Alex North
Arranged by Carol Klose

Slowly, with expression (♩ = 92)

Oh, my love, my dar - ling, I've hun - gered for your

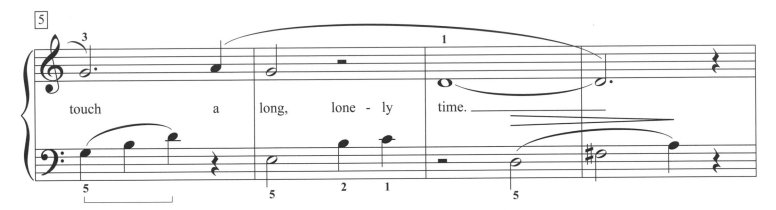

touch a long, lone - ly time.

Time goes by so slow - ly and time can do so

Accompaniment (Student plays one octave higher than written.)

Slowly, with expression (♩ = 92)

With pedal

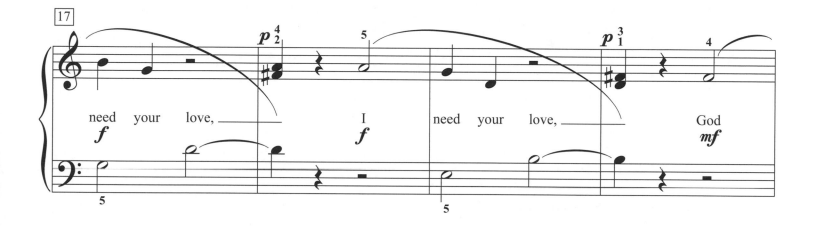

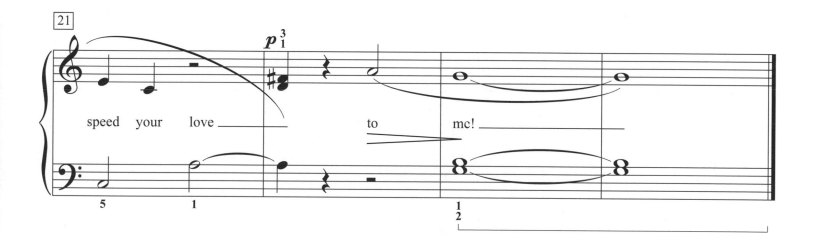

What I Did for Love

from A CHORUS LINE

Music by Marvin Hamlisch
Lyric by Edward Kleban
Arranged by Fred Kern

love, what I did for love. _____ Look, my eyes are

mf

dry, _____ the gift was ours to bor - row. _____

_____ It's as if we al - ways knew, _____

_____ But I won't for - get what I did for love, what I did for

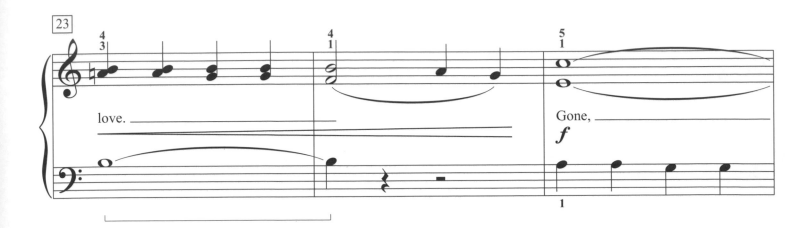

love. _____ Gone, _____

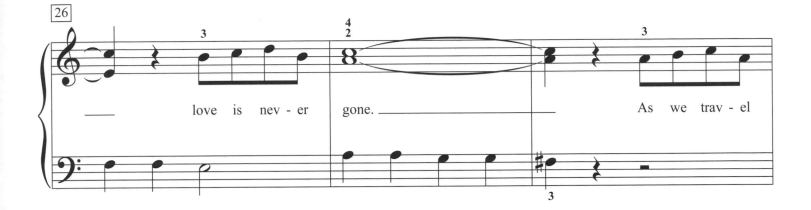

_____ love is nev - er gone. _____ As we trav - el

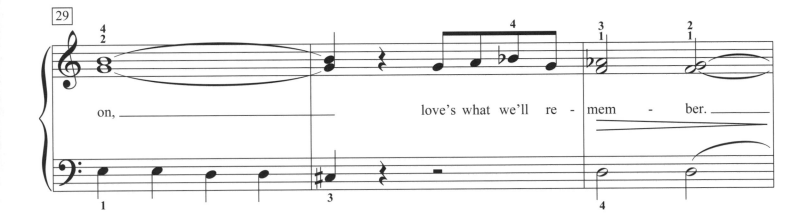

on, _____ love's what we'll re - mem - ber. _____

Kiss to - day good - bye, _____ and point me t'ward to -

mor - row. _____ We did what we had to do. _____

_____ Won't for - get, can't re - gret what I did for

(cross over)

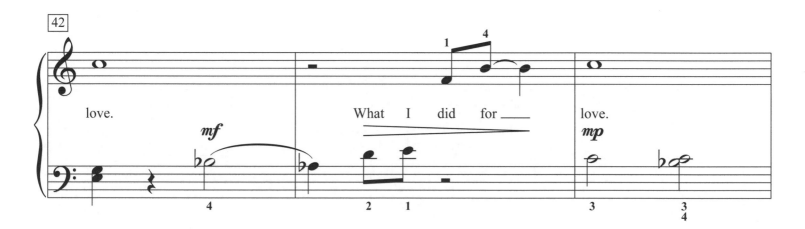

love. What I did for ____ love.

Both hands 8va

What I did for ____ love.

A Whole New World

from ALADDIN

Music by Alan Menken
Lyrics by Tim Rice
Arranged by Carol Klose

I can show you the world,
shin - ing, shim - mer - ing,

I can o - pen your eyes,
take you won - der by

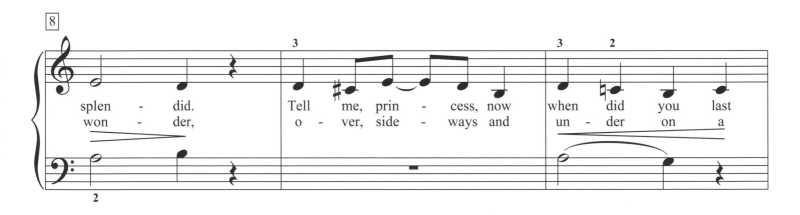

splen - did.
Tell me, prin - cess, now
when did you last

won - der,
o - ver, side - ways and
un - der on a

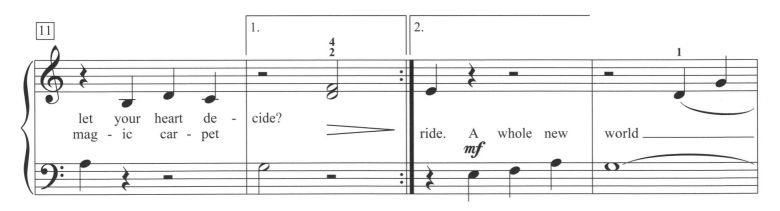

let your heart de - cide?

mag - ic car - pet
ride. A whole new world

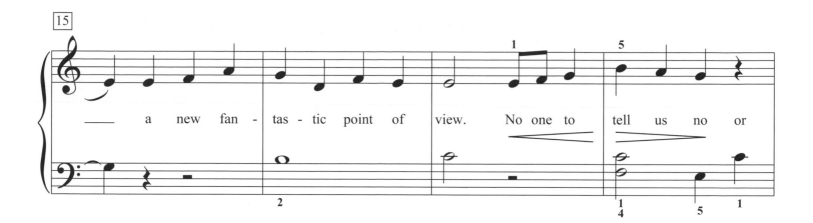

_____ a new fan - tas - tic point of view. No one to tell us no or

where to go or say we're on - ly dream - ing. A whole new world, _____

_____ a daz - zling place I nev - er knew. But when I'm way up here, it's

crys - tal clear that now I'm in a whole new world with you.

What a Wonderful World

Words and Music by George David Weiss
and Bob Thiele
Arranged by Mona Rejino

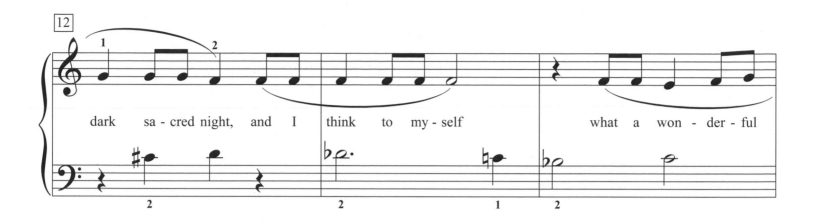

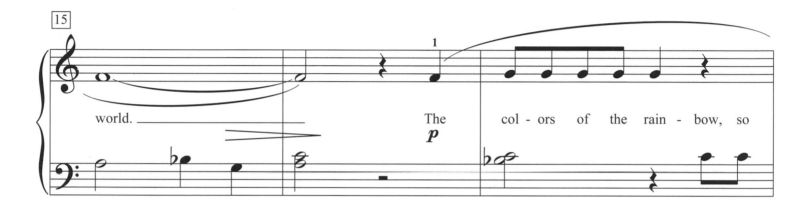

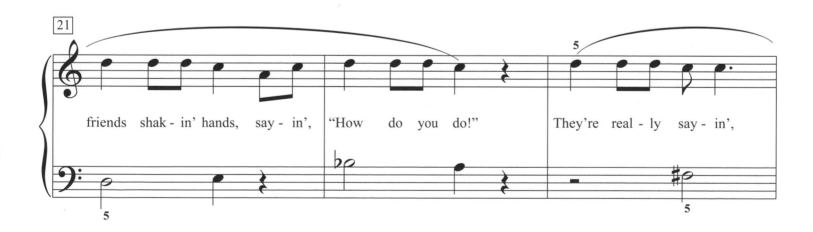

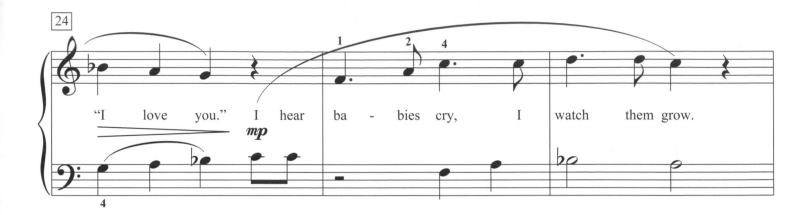

"I love you." I hear ba - bies cry, I watch them grow.

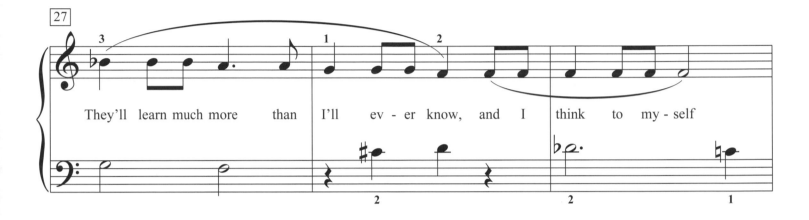

They'll learn much more than I'll ev - er know, and I think to my - self

what a won - der - ful world. _____ Yes, I

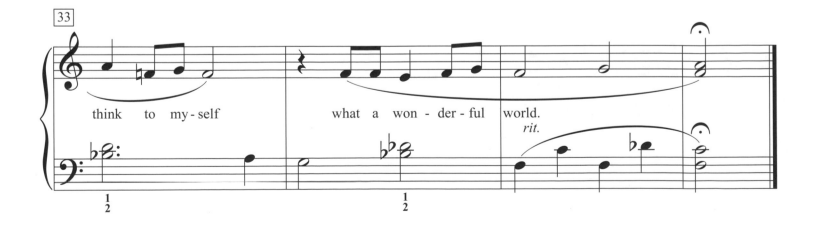

think to my - self what a won - der - ful world.

142